SEX DIFFERENCES

SEX DIFFERENCES

Modern Biology and the Unisex Fallacy

Yves Christen

Translated by

Nicholas Davidson

Transaction Publishers
New Brunswick (U.S.A.) and London (U.K.)

Library of Congress Catalog Number: 90-11196
ISBN: 0-88738-869-8
Printed in the United States of America

        Library of Congress Cataloging-in-Publication Data
Christen, Yves.
        [Égalité des sexes. English]
        Sex differences: modern biology and the unisex fallacy / Yves
        Christen; translated by Nicholas Davidson.
                p. cm.
        Translation of: L'Égalité des sexes.
        Includes bibliographical references (p.) and index.
        ISBN 0-88738-869-8
        1. Sex differences (Psychology) 2. Sex differences.
                3rd. Feminism.
I. Title
BF692.2.C4713 1990   90-11196
155.3'3--dc20   CIP

Contents

Introduction   1

1. Differences and Similarities   3

2. An Unexpected Feminism   7

3. The Weaker Sex Is Not the One You Think   21

4. The Two Sexual Strategies   29

5. The Descent of Woman   37

6. Hierarchy and Gender   49

7. The Pirandello Effect   57

8. Sex Differences in Brain Structure   65

9. The Circle of Life   81

10. Proof by Pathology   87

11. Male and Female Modalities   95

12. Toward Feminitude?   109

Bibliography   119

Index   139

Introduction

In a sense, it's all been said. Women and men are equal, but they differ in almost every way possible; there is an innate female nature, but only woman's subject status explains the existence of masculinity and femininity; all the deplored inequalities will disappear when the struggle for women's liberation achieves its goals, but there is a kind of fate in this area. To Simone de Beauvoir's celebrated assertion that "one is not born, but rather becomes, a woman," Evelyne Sullerot replies, "One is indeed born a woman," and Odette Thibaut responds in turn, "One is born, and also becomes, a woman" (30, 351, 363).*

Yes, it's all been said—and even a little more, so rich is the catalogue of folly in this area. Our century of ideological confrontation had hardly begun when Dr. P.J. Moebius published his book on "physiological mental debility in woman" and Otto Weininger his very antifeminist *Sex and Character*. Just yesterday Françoise d'Eaubonne, feeling bound to give her feminism the anti-genetic tone of a Lysenko, proclaimed that "The idea of a human behavior determined by certain chromosomes is old-fashioned!" In reality, here as elsewhere, the extremists answer each other, with the absurdities of some justifying those of the rest.

That it's all been said, that every opinion has been emitted and every absurdity uttered, does not signify that the essential has been explained. Nor does it signify that the importance of the debate has been properly understood, any more than has the width of the chasm that is opening between an idea that is currently translating itself through acts and a toddling knowledge that is challenging the conventional wisdom.

This paradoxical situation, moreover, is not entirely unique. Such, in effect, is the destiny of ideologies: the moment they gain official status is the moment they appear completely obsolete. Very often academic consecration is just a promotion to irrelevancy, a way to clear away dead ideas.

*The numbers in parentheses refer to the bibliography at the end of the book.

Henceforth, sexism is prohibited—punished like racism by the laws. Of course, "sexism" refers to something ambiguous—laws are never perfectly clear; they apply to a human reality that, necessarily, is nuanced—but it signifies, in any case, something that involves a recognition or cultivation of the differences between men and women. It is a matter, to simplify somewhat, of conferring official status on a certain kind of feminism, that propounded by Simone de Beauvoir in *The Second Sex*—a perfectly clear ideology that Sartre's companion summarized without nuance:

First, man made woman into the Other, the object.

Second, there is no female nature. The entire Feminine is artificial.

These ideas have since taken their course. They have influenced writers, male and female, and inspired politicians. They have also challenged a handful of writers and researchers, who have published their conclusions over the past few years and continue to flood us with new findings. From their various specialties have come several pounds of literature that is mostly technical and, as one would expect, often contradictory. But though many points remain obscure, certain conclusions are already visible. Arguably, these conclusions do not address every possible form of feminism, but in any case they demolish the philosophy of Simone de Beauvoir, which currently commands political support but has lost the support of science. After years of being promoted by intellectuals hostile to the political powers, this philosophy increasingly finds itself with political power for its only support.

To take the measure of the existing paradox, and introduce a modicum of order to a debate where the received ideas are winning out too often—such are some of the ambitions of the present work.

But we would also like to go a little further: to renounce a few simplistic ideas and—why not?—advocate a different kind of feminism, that which consists in viewing woman as something other than a near-equal of man—a being who, by trying to be the same as her model, can hope at most to rival, but not truly to equal him. There are differences between men and women. To deny this is not only futile but could well be damaging to the female cause. What is at stake here is the uniqueness of the two partners, male and female, and not the eulogy of their similarities, which only trivializes them.

1

Differences and Similarities

According to Jean Cau, man and woman resemble each other when they are two skeletons. This is both true and false. It is true in that the differences between the sexes are so great that only the influence of fashion and the prejudices of a conformism that regards itself as anti-conformism prevent a grasp of their scope. But it is also false, and even doubly so: first, because even as skeletons the two sexes are still different (if only in terms of the pelvic bones); second, and in the opposite sense, because men and women are nevertheless very much alike.

An Attenuated Sexual Dimorphism

Members of the same species, Homo sapiens, they share the majority of their physical and even psychological characteristics. From hair structure to blood groups and the functioning of the various organs, in most respects, one observes sameness or at least resemblance. Moreover, sexual dimorphism, or the physical difference between the sexes, has diminished in the course of human evolution (75, 133).

The male baboon is much larger than the female baboon. He possesses giant canine teeth, true weapons, whose purpose is to assure his domination of the troop and, in particular, of its females. Nothing comparable is found in man. Furnished with a penis significantly larger than that of the other great apes and with large testicles (though smaller than those of the male chimpanzee), he is certainly a little larger and stronger than the female (who herself enjoys an exceptionally large pair of breasts for a primate), but the overall difference between the sexes does not approach that found in the gorilla or orangutan.

This kind of fact should be kept in mind when investigating the extent of sex differences: first, so as not to exaggerate them; but also because that which is no longer physically apparent may be compensated for in some other way.

Another fundamental fact that should not be ignored, on pain of flirting with misunderstanding, is that genetically speaking, men and women are manifestly very similar. Out of a total of 46 chromosomes (the tiny threads that make up the physical armature of heredity), only one differs between men and women. In other words, if one seeks, as we do here, to evaluate the influence of genetic factors on human beings, is is important to bear in mind that the makeup of the two sexes is very similar in this regard.

At the same time, it is also necessary not to rest content with elementary arithmetic in this area. Beings whose genetic differences are very slight can appear to be very different. For instance, a condition such as mongoloidism, which is caused by the presence of a single extra chromosome (number 21), manifests itself in a major set of anomalies. An even smaller genetic upset can affect many physical and psychological traits. It is therefore permissible to conceive that the various particularities associated with gender, and notably the hormonal ones, suffice to permeate many aspects of the human body and mind.

The Decline of Distinct Sex Roles

Having said as much, we must once more insist on the reality of the similarities between the sexes, and also on the fact that very few tasks are linked exclusively to either sex. There are now female pilots, engineers, astronauts, executives, cabinet officials, scientists, bullfighters, etc.

Similarly, men increasingly perform tasks that were once almost exclusively female: infant care, childrearing, and various household chores. There are even male nurses and midwives.

There is no doubt that women, or at least some women, can perform almost all tasks performed by men and vice versa, with the conspicuous exception of childbearing. But even this absolute difference between the sexes no longer has the impact formerly attributed to it. For example, the sociologist Herbert Spencer, conceiving of the human being as a sort of reservoir of energy, concluded that a woman who developed her intellectual qualities was perforce obliged to sacrifice her mothering role. Lacking an infinite amount of energy, every other task was a dispersion or waste of energy. It was not a question, one should note, of denying women's qualities—Spencer believed that women could be at least as intelligent as men—but of presenting them with a choice: either to develop their individual qualities or to have children. This opposition long prevailed—the development of woman versus the reproductive imperative. It persists today in that, for example, it is difficult for a woman both to have numerous children and to pursue a professional career. But social evolution has provided a number of palliatives to this difficulty.

If all this is true, one may ask: Why write a book about the differences between men and women, rather than one about their similarities? It is the old question of whether the glass is half full or half empty. Why give pride of place to the differences? The answer is simply that it is the differences which originalize. The similarities between the sexes are indeed a reality. But it is an insignificant reality, a sort of background noise devoid of consequence. That is why we have chosen to emphasize the differences here. For they alone carry meaning.

2

An Unexpected Feminism

In 1985, Algerian women began going to the movies again. The government had decided they could attend special reserved screenings. Before this decision, the men had created such a ruckus over their presence that the women eventually deserted the dimly lit theaters altogether.

This story is worth pausing over. Like many ordinary events, it is extraordinarily charged with meaning. On one hand, it attests to the survival of sexism and machismo. On the other, the solution chosen invites further reflection. What does it amount to, in effect, if not a sort of apartheid? It certainly bears no resemblance to the declared antisexism of today's feminists. It was not by an excess of egalitarianism, of uniformity, that it was possible to allow Algerian women to return to the cinemas, but rather by recognizing them as women—that is, as beings different from men.

Is the solution adopted fully satisfactory? Surely not. Manifestly, logic and simple good sense indicate that men and women should be able to occupy the same physical space without starting a riot. But mentalities are not like objects that can easily be pushed aside—and doubtless that of the North African male less than all others. For this reason, a lesser evil was chosen. This is what is called realism.

In a sense, the entire female question is enclosed within this incident. For it illustrates the essential point: after years of official feminism—particularly in intellectual milieus—men and women continue to live as different beings. They still practice a certain kind of discrimination; and only an acknowledgment of differences makes it possible, if not to end it, then at least to adapt to it.

The Failure of Egalitarian Feminism

That machismo persists more or less everywhere can hardly be denied.* In May 1985, the tale of *The Thousand and One Nights* was declared a pornographic work in Egypt, where, under the influence of integrism, women's rights have long been abrogated.

Even in Western lands, where the status of women appears to be more satisfactory, discrimination persists in various areas: unjustified differences in wages, sexual harassment in the workplace, etc.

In France, a government ministry on the status of women has been established to combat these unjustified inequalities, and it has been decided to classify sexism and racism as a single entity. This idea derives directly from the feminism of the 1960s. It affirms as official truth that men and women do not differ significantly and that in consequence the proscribed thesis must disappear. But what can we expect at the level of facts?

To learn the answer to this question, it suffices to examine the events of recent history. It is only a few decades since women acquired the right to vote in Western lands. Female candidates subsequently campaigned for office and some were in fact elected. But has the proportion of women going into politics noticeably and steadily increased? Not in the least. Similarly, the number of women with cabinet rank has remained very small and the number of women in cabinet-level positions unrelated to feminine activities (the family, the status of women) is still infinitesimal. Neither the various declarations of intent nor the assorted measures taken have managed to set woman more firmly on the route of Homo politicus.

Another example, more localized in space and time, is the Israeli kibbutz, whose policies are deliberately egalitarian, antisexist, and nonfamilial. These policies have failed. Women have remained women and mothers have remained mothers.

One could go on indefinitely citing the things that have not changed as well as those that have—the right to vote, abortion, contraception, more equitable wage policies, etc. In a sense, the score may seem to indicate a draw: some things change and others stay the same (41). But how can we fail to see that what does *not* change in all this is the relationship between man and woman? To take one example out of a

*Cf. 6, 33, 81, 101, 109, 110, 130, 142, 170, 193, 199, 203, 223, 227, 241, 268, 273, 274, 286, 288, 290, 293, 299, 314, 327, 352, 363.

thousand: if the most unjustified wage differences are being eliminated, it is no less true that men still earn more than women on average
and tend to occupy the highest-ranking positions.* In 1973, an article
on the wage gap was entitled "A Woman is 58% of a Man" (204). Ten
years later, things had barely changed, and a different writer could echo
that "a woman is 59% of a man" (264). Why this persisting discrimination? Is it a result of ingrained sexist habits? No doubt it is, at least
in part. But how can we explain the habits themselves? For if sexism
covers the earth to such an extent, there must be some reason for it.

The error of 1960s feminism is precisely to reject all inquiry concerning this point. This denial makes it appear as if sexism must come
from the Holy Ghost or sheer chance.

Mentalities are Hardy Creatures

More significant still is the question of stereotypes, those one-sided
ideas that circulate about men and women—the eternal feminine, the
eternal masculine, and similar retrograde schemas, which everyone
agrees are ridiculous! After several decades of feminism, at a time
when fashions have in fact substantially changed, often in the direction
of unisexism, have these notions actually evolved in the same way?
That would at least appear plausible. That is exactly what has not hap-
pened (56, 311).

A poll of a large sample of Americans of both sexes and all ages
attests this very clearly. Three-quarters of those questioned agreed with
the stereotypes on sex differences, including the most debatable and
those that one might have thought were dated or even ridiculous.

Thus, on a test involving 41 stereotypes, 28 corresponding to the
masculine pole were characterized as desirable: very aggressive, very
independent, not at all emotional, almost always hides emotions, very
objective, not at all easily influenced, very dominant, likes math and
science very much, not at all excitable in a minor crisis, very active,
very competitive, very logical, very worldly, very skilled in business,
very direct, knows the way of the world, feelings not easily hurt, very
adventurous, can make decisions easily, never cries, almost always acts
as a leader, very self-confident, not at all uncomfortable about being
aggressive, very ambitious, easily able to separate feelings from ideas,
not at all dependent, never conceited about appearance, thinks men are

*Cf. 37, 45, 148, 208.

always superior to women, and talks freely with men about sex: this is how the male appears in terms of his positive qualities in the eyes of both men and women today. The model woman is defined by the opposite traits—from "very unaggressive" to "does not talk freely with men about sex"—in addition to 18 others on which the feminine pole is considered superior. She doesn't use harsh language, is very talkative, very tactful, very gentle, very aware of the feelings of others, very religious, very interested in her own appearance, very neat in her habits, very quiet, has a very strong need for security, enjoys art and literature, and easily expresses tender feelings. On this occasion, the masculine pole is characterized by the opposite traits (56).

Thus, the matter is clear: not only have stereotypes not changed (the same traits are still considered masculine or feminine), not only are the masculine stereotypes still ranked higher than the feminine ones, but the members of both sexes share the same views in this area (56). This is certainly not to conclude that the stereotypes are accurate—quite the contrary. Moreover, what matters here is not whether they are true or false but that they are considered to be true by the overwhelming majority of those questioned, at a time when the social environment, media opinion, and intellectual and political fashions have in fact evolved. Apparently, everything takes place as though the ideas expressed in this area had changed completely—but not the mentalities. In this regard the feminism of the 1960s, while achieving a certain success in the political sphere, has been ineffective. Henceforth, we will have to reverse the usual perspective, which presents sexism as something unnatural that is produced by convention or socialization. Clearly, it is antisexism that rests on the superficial, the abstract, and the inauthentic.

Machismo and 1960s-style Feminism: Two Objective Allies

To recognize the differences between the sexes, at the risk of escaping the ambit of the banal, the fashionable, and the habitual, invites us to reflect on their extent and origins. The sort of explanation that rests content with phrases such as "If men and women are still different, it's because the former have exploited the latter for a long time" amounts at best to an interpretation on the order of "If you get fat, it's because you eat too much." Such an explanation, of course, avoids an inquiry into the causes of overeating and into the fact that all those who overeat do not gain the same amount of weight. If one sex has subordinated the other—a notion that is partly correct but also notoriously exaggerated—it is because from the beginning there has existed a sort of *dissymmetry* in the relations of the two members of the couple: they do not use the same weapons or fill the same functions. For this reason, if one wishes to organize a duel between them, one should not choose the weapons of the dominant partner. In plain language, it is a mistake to try to show that women are identical to men.

Perhaps we should even call into question the grounds for the duel altogether—in this case, the effort to identify one sex with the other. From this point of view, *machismo and 1960s-style feminism are two sides of the same coin. They represent partners in crime locked in the dialogue of equality-inequality.* Although they differ in their conclusions, they agree on the terms of debate. Moreover, the claims of one sustain the conclusions of the other. In a sense, only the excesses committed on both sides justify the continued existence of these opposing camps.

From this perspective, it is a question of a schematization, an impoverishment of intellectual debate not far removed from children's squabbles: "My daddy's stronger than your daddy!" "No, my daddy's stronger than your daddy!"

Impoverishment. The word is even more justified when one considers the origins of the feminist movement. A current of thought favorable to the emancipation of women can be traced to that moment of transition in which the intellectual scuffles of the last century toppled into the ideological conflicts of our own time. It was not, to be sure, an organized movement, a party, but rather a loose confederation of pluralistic ideas, with its own points of reference, which maintained close ties with the other "isms" that were gestating around the same time: Marxism, Darwinism, and sexualism (if one can so call the study of one of the great taboo subjects). In the shadow of Marx, Darwin, and Havelock Ellis emerged several female figures who are often forgotten or poorly known today—perhaps because their way of thinking does not accord with the schematizations of our own time; or perhaps because their feminism was not synonymous with egalitarianism, with the renunciation of femininity.

Clémence Royer, "Almost a Man of Genius"

Among these female figures fascinated by science and feminism, one of the most remarkable is the Frenchwoman Clémence Royer

(1830-1902). A philosopher and scientist, Clémence Royer was first and foremost a creature devoted to liberty. She was self-taught, indefatigable, and immensely cultivated. Her works cover fields as diverse as tax policy, anthropology, morality, and astronomy. Ernest Renan, impressed by her learning, is supposed to have made the execrable remark that she was "almost a man of genius."

Fascinated by Darwin's theory, Clémence Royer was the first to translate his *Origin of Species* into French. She prefaced the work with an introduction, written in a very personal vein, which does not merely expound the work but in some regards looks beyond it, as in her remarks on the evolution of man. For Clémence Royer, it was already clear that the transformist theory must apply to the emergence of our own species. To this end, she undertook a work on "The Origin of Man and Society," which appeared in 1869, one year before *The Descent of Man*, in which the great British biologist extended his vision to the human species. It seems likely, as she herself reports, that her pretensions as a translator caused considerable friction with Darwin, who rejected her collaboration on future editions with the complaint that she had published the third edition without taking his revisions into account.

A fount of culture, Clémence Royer was also a feminist and an advocate of free love. She participated in the first feminist congress in 1878 and, with fifteen other people, founded the first sexually integrated Masonic lodge in 1893. Also in 1893, the leading French feminist journal offered to support her as a feminist political candidate—a proposal that she turned down. Yet, although not a militant committed to any single movement, Clémence Royer was thoroughly engaged. She called for a wide variety of reforms, starting with a proposal that unmarried women no longer be addressed as "Miss."

But though Clémence Royer was an advocate of equality, was she an egalitarian? This was plainly not the case, as her own statements make clear. As she said in one of her speeches,

> I believe that in everything she does, a woman must remain herself. I have always disliked the servile imitation of men by women, in both art and literature, and I would go so far as to criticize it in science. Other than the fact that I cannot abide imitations of any sort, whether of works or persons, we have our own particular genius as women and should be careful to preserve it, and even to develop its particular tendencies, rather than attempting to conceal and eradicate it. It is one more register in the great organ of nature's harmonies. If it is to be in tune with the uni-

versal concert, it must retain its own pitch and tonality. We should differ in spirit as we do in appearance, and be in all things a being equal and analogous to man, without ever attempting to become identical to him. (124, p. 106)

This vision is similar to the philosophy she expounds in her introduction to Darwin's work, which is both very personal and very inegalitarian. "Men are unequal by nature," she asserts (306, p. 38). In her hands, this viewpoint comes across as simultaneously extreme and nuanced:

[Men] are individually unequal, even among the purest races.

These inequalities assume such massive proportions between different races in terms of intellect that the legislator should always take them into account. But, on the other hand, these individual and contingent differences can be erased, can disappear little by little, can dissolve into a thousand intermediate nuances; so that the theory of natural selection, applied to the social sciences, mandates as much against the regime of distinct, closed, static classes as against the regime of absolute equality.

Thus, developing her thought in the footsteps of mid-nineteenth-century Darwinism, Clémence Royer combined inegalitarianism and the desire for social justice in a single theme, careful to confuse nothing. Her conclusion is logical, in a sense, if one views selection as all-powerful, in which case it would suffice to allow competition to occur. Clémence Royer thereby distances herself from socialism. Karl Marx realized this very well, though not his son-in-law Paul Lafargue, who tried to contact the translator of Darwin. He was rebuffed, to Marx's immense satisfaction (70, 225).

As the proponent of a biologizing vision of life and society, Clémence Royer very clearly articulates what her feminism represents from that perspective: a power over life by means of maternity. In her view, women should receive financial support as mothers. As she wrote:

As soon as a woman becomes a mother, her most real and important work is her children's upbringing, and she does well to devote herself to it entirely, provided that her individual aptitudes incline her to it naturally. This work which costs her and produces nothing for her, this work whose sole beneficiary is society, for which she raises new citizens, is a sufficient contribution. No man renders a greater service to the State except when he gives his life on the battlefield. Motherhood is women's military service. (308)

Alice Lee and the Female Brain

If Darwinism excited few female brains in late nineteenth-century France, the situation was very different in England. Under the dual banner of science and socialism, feminists were organizing. The Men and Women's Club, for instance, included the sexologist Havelock Ellis, the biologist Karl Pearson, and such women as Eleanor Marx, Annie Besant, Olive Schreiner, and Mrs. Wilson. If the shadow of Karl Marx was not far away, his own daughter being a member of the group, that of the eugenicists was closer still through the presence of Karl Pearson. Pearson was the successor of Francis Galton, the founder of this new discipline, whose object is to improve the genetic potential of populations. Pearson, a socialist, eugenicist, and feminist, was one of the first to open his laboratory to women, first to Dr. Alice Lee (1859–1939) and subsequently to Dr. Ethel Elderton (1878–1954).

Alice Lee was the first woman to graduate from the University of London, obtaining her B.Sc. in 1884. She first met Pearson, her future mentor, through an exchange of letters in 1892. At the time, she was an assistant teacher of mathematics and physics but was also participating in the teaching of Latin and Greek. Pearson thought her efforts were too dispersed—a rather strange judgment coming from a man who was himself simultaneously involved in mathematics, biology, and philosophy.

Fascinated by the statistical work of Galton's heir-apparent, Alice Lee participated in the laboratory studies in biometry while attending Pearson's courses. Scientists at this time displayed an immoderate taste for cranial measurements. It was rather generally acknowledged that the races and sexes differed markedly in this regard. Thus, whites were reputed to have a greater cranial capacity than blacks and men a greater cranial capacity than women.

Although she accepted the first of these claims, Alice Lee attacked the second one. This question was viewed as a major scientific issue at the time. In 1881, the French ethnologist Letourneau claimed to have established that women's cranial capacity was less than men's. To refute him, Alice Lee developed a formula for measuring the cranial capacity of living subjects. She used this new formula at a conference of the Anatomical Society held in Dublin in 1898. The subjects of her study were the thirty-five male anatomists present. After having duly measured all of their skulls, she ranked them in decreasing order of cranial capacity. Her future examiner, Sir William Turner, found himself in eighth place, not very pleased and already prepared to admit that the correlation between cranial capacity and intelligence was not as significant as previously thought. Worse still, Karl Pearson himself placed near the bottom. The last of all was J. Kollman, "one of the ablest living anthropologists," according to Alice Lee (which has not prevented him from being completely forgotten today: did his cranial measurements unmask the imposture?). In addition to these individual cases, there were major differences in averages: the first eighteen anatomists had an average capacity of 1,601 cubic centimeters, in contrast to 1,468 cc for the last seventeen. "He would be a bold man," wrote Alice Lee, "who would assert that there is a substantial average superiority in the first half" (196, p. 255). Not wishing to deny the importance of all structural differences, she proposed that the principal variable might involve the cerebral convolutions.

With experiments like this, Alice Lee encountered some difficulty in obtaining an advanced degree. The mathematician J. Larmor, a member of her doctoral committee, was especially hostile, claiming that Lee had merely continued Pearson's work and ideas. Pearson denied this and appealed to Galton himself to defend her. Now, Galton was a firm believer in female intellectual inferiority. Nevertheless, he agreed to meet with the candidate. Before this important encounter, Pearson gave his student the usual advice. "Mr. Francis Galton. . . is not an ogre," he told her, but, "as Sir William Turner, he [argues] from the absolute size of men and women's brains. . . . Point out *humorously* to Mr. Galton where he comes on your list. Don't do it, however, as if you objected to him as an examiner" (210, p. 178). The meeting took place on July 1, 1899.

Alice Lee wrote to Pearson the next day. She had met with Galton over tea, and "he was extremely kind" (70).

But Galton would hear nothing of the substance of the question. Anyone who has undergone a doctoral examination, whether in easy circumstances or not, will readily grasp the piquant and tragic aspects of this situation. The University of London finally granted Alice Lee a doctorate in 1901. But the struggle had been a bitter one. And all the influence of Pearson, the eugenicist, the social Darwinist, had been necessary to achieve this female academic triumph.

For the rest, it must be said that Alice Lee unflinchingly accepted the notion of "racial types" developed by Pearson and that she participated in the work of his eugenics laboratory from 1895 until her retirement in 1927, and mostly as a volunteer. Pearson never abandoned her—she who had given so much of her life to eugenics research. In 1923, he obtained for her a pension of 70 pounds a year, writing to the British Home Office that "few, if any woman workers of her period have accomplished such a bulk of first class research as Dr. Lee" (210, p. 152).

The other leading woman in the eugenics movement, Ethel Elderton, studied the heredity of intelligence and the effects of parental alcoholism (105). In 1905, she began work at the Eugenics Record Office, where she remained until 1933. "Of all the women of the eugenics laboratory," says her biographer Rosaleen Love, it was she "who did most to wear down Francis Galton's prejudice that women were intuitive unintellectual creatures incapable of sound academic work" (210, p. 152). As a eugenicist, Ethel Elderton could only deplore the decline in the British birth rate and insist on the importance of women in any policy of genetic amelioration.

Neither Alice Lee nor Ethel Elderton can be assimilated to today's socialists. But in their time, they represented the avant-garde of feminism. Theirs was a feminism that, very clearly, did not seek to deny the differences between men and women but to validate them. And they did so in the name of the community's interest. Thus, when Olive Schreiner called for work for women, she said that "We demand this, not for ourselves alone, but for the race" (325, p. 27).*

Margaret Sanger: Birth Control and the Defense of Civilization

In the United States, scientifically inspired feminism drew on the same sources and spoke in the same tones as in Europe. Margaret Sanger, a heroine of the movement for woman's liberation, was also an inspirational symbol to eugenicist groups (136, 371).

Sanger, president of the Birth Control League and editor until 1929 of its publication, *The Birth Control Review,* was the principal

---

*This controversial South African writer occupied an interesting place in the intellectual debates of her time. A friend of the genetician Pearson and the sexologist Ellis, she was doubtless partly responsible for the conflicts between these two thinkers, both of them elitists and eugenicists, and, in particular, for their conflict over the postulated greater variability of women than men, a theory put forward by Ellis and immediately attacked by Pearson. An acrimonious exchange followed, which no doubt owed much to a rivalry between the two men over Olive Schreiner. Ellis seems to have been madly in love with her, but she herself was in love with Pearson (61, 337).

American figure in the movement for birth control. An exceptionally dynamic person, she published a monthly magazine, *The Woman Rebel*, and was the author of several books, including among others *What Every Girl Should Know, The Case for Birth Control, The Pivot of Civilization,* and *Happiness in Marriage.* She organized the first international convention on world population, held in Geneva in 1927.

Born into the working class, a member as of 1912 of the Socialist Party, where she undertook the task of recruiting women from the workers' clubs of New York, Margaret Sanger had many firsthand opportunities to witness concrete misery, notably that caused by a lack of contraceptive knowledge. In her autobiography, she relates the circumstances that led her to throw herself into this struggle. She was visiting Sadie Sachs, a 28-year-old woman who had attempted an abortion. When, in visible despair, the patient asked the doctor for advice, he told her to send her husband to sleep under the roof! Margaret Sanger wrote:

> I glanced quickly at Mrs. Sachs. Even through my sudden tears I could see stamped on her face despair. We simply looked at each other, saying no word until the door had closed behind the doctor. Then she lifted her thin, blue-veined hands and clasped them beseechingly: "He can't understand. He's only a man. But you do, don't you? Please tell me the secret, and I'll never breathe it to a soul. *Please!*" (318, p. 91)

Three months later Sadie Sachs was dead, the victim of another attempted abortion. The next morning, after having passed a sleepless night, Margaret Sanger decided to fight, to try "to do something to change the destiny of mothers whose miseries were as vast as the sky" (318, p. 92).

To liberate woman through the practice of contraception: such was Margaret Sanger's mission. But this struggle, which is waged from an individualist standpoint today, was in her case waged in the name of civilization. Viewing men and women as members of "one great organism," Margaret Sanger denounced individualism and egoism. She saw herself as concerned with "the 'seeds' of civilization." Mothers, she says, should no longer regard themselves as slaves but liberate themselves through the exercise of their own intelligence; in a word, they must "become *civilized*" (317, pp. 525–527). To be civilized is to seek to increase intelligence, to invoke Montesquieu's idea of the parallel between intelligence and civilization. This is to be accomplished through birth control, practiced from a eugenic point of view (cf. 62).

To be sure, Margaret Sanger was well aware that she would encounter opposition from reactionary quarters. As for the socialists with whom she had long been associated, they had little interest in the female condition or birth control. The revolutionary in this area was Margaret Sanger, who denounced the reactionary "'morality'" defended by the Church, against which "the spirit of Western civilization is revolting with ever-increasing vigor" (317, p. 532).

It was necessary, according to Sanger, to encourage reproduction among high-quality couples and condemn miscegenation. From this point of view, she asserted, contraception needs no further justification: "it is a force for civilization in itself." For this American feminist, such was the logical outcome of the liberation movement:

> Women in the past have been confronted with the empty victories of political freedom, of economic freedom, of social freedom. But with the winning of *biological freedom*, women and men and children will enter triumphantly into an era that will be in every sense of the word civilized. (317, p. 537)

From Women's Liberation to Women's Validation

As the struggles of these three women indicate—Clémence Royer in France, Alice Lee in Britain, Margaret Sanger in the United States—feminism has not aimed solely to minimize the existence of sex differences, and still less to make woman into a near–man.

Today it is easy to identify the errors in the theories of these three women. But these theories must be viewed in the context of their time. Certainly, they contain some extremely dubious ideas. But that is not the important point here. These biologizing feminists justified their struggle on the basis of their sex's utility. They did so not from an individualist standpoint but in the name of society, race, and civilization. The tenor of these criteria may be irritating. But one should above all note what they imply with regard to gender: an idea that is validating for women—namely, that woman is sufficiently perfected to play an important social role and not merely to take pleasure. There is nothing as validating as this in the demands of 1960s-style feminism. Intending to unburden woman, these end up making her more available to herself and man. And, in point of fact, the use of the pill may have presented the greatest advantages to the most macho of Don Juans. Far be it from me to despise the quest for happiness and comfort. But how can one fail to see that to emphasize this preoccupation so exclusively is in itself devalidating for women? In plain language, it amounts to setting up the following equation: to men and women alike the quest for sexual pleasure; to men alone the task of accomplishing a social role, of behaving like civilized beings. That is why, beneath the verbal excesses proper to precursors, the Clémence Royers, Alice Lees, and Margaret Sangers must in reality be regarded as the pioneers not only of the movement for women's liberation, but also of the movement leading to women's validation—a movement that may reveal itself to be infinitely less archaic than it seems. Does it not touch on the central notion of feminism, whether this is acknowledged or not?—namely, that women, more than men, hold the destiny of civilizations in their hands, for, more than men, they hold genetic power. This is what the feminist biologist Sarah Hrdy expresses when she says that women hold a genetic right of veto. Even more striking, a similar analysis has been arrived at by Germaine Greer, ultrafeminist author of *The Female Eunuch* (1970). In her more recent book *Sex and Destiny* (1984), sex ceases to be primarily a subject for demands; it is the vector of the destiny of civilizations via the intermediary of procreation (in the event, a sign of the decline of Western peoples, victims of their insufficient desire for reproduction) (138). Clearly, from whatever pole one starts, a feminist analysis, if even modestly elaborated, sooner or later ends by recognizing the link between femininity and civilization.

3

The Weaker Sex Is Not the One You Think

"The truly feminine woman," writes Nietzsche, "rejects, tooth and nail, every form of 'rights.' The state of nature, the incessant war between the sexes, easily assures her of the supremacy." Science has confirmed the German philosopher: the weaker sex is not the one people think it is. And this is not a matter of some vague condescension but of an avalanche of new biological and demographic information.

The Longevity Gap

There is, first of all, the following fact: women live longer than men (282, 339, 396). In France, the reports of the INED (Institut National d'Etudes Démographiques) show that the gap in this area is actually increasing. In 1982, life expectancy was 71 years for men versus 79 years for women, a gap of 8 years, versus 5.5 years in 1946–49. While men attained a life expectancy of 65 a full 9 years later than their companions (in 1954 versus 1946), their handicap reached 20 years for a life expectancy of 69 (1970 versus 1950). With regard to a life expectancy of 70 years, the so-called weaker sex reached it in 1952, whereas the male sex has barely reached it after a delay of nearly 30 years.

Similar figures are recorded for most Western countries. In the United States, the average longevity of white women was 77.7 years in 1977 versus 70 years for men—a gap of 7.7, compared to a gap of 2.9 recorded in 1900 (48.2 years for men and 51.1 years for women).

It is extremely striking that male over-mortality occurs in all age groups. Fortunately for demographic equilibrium, significantly more boys are born than girls; for from birth onward, the majority sex pays a heavy tribute to disease of all kinds. Under age one, the mortality ratio is 1.26—for every 100 girl babies who die, 126 boy babies die; between the ages of one and four the mortality ratio is 1.29; between five and 14 it is 1.44; between 15 and 24 it is 3.11; between 25 and 34 it is 2.64; between 35 and 44 it is 1.93; between 45 and 54 it is 1.90; between 55 and 64 it is 1.95; between 65 and 74 it is 1.93; between 75 and 84 it is 1.65; and after 85 it is 1.25 (396).

These figures should not be regarded as merely anecdotal. They reflect an important social reality: *our world is becoming feminized as it grows older*. Thus, among Americans over 65 in 1979, there were 138 women for every 100 men. A corollary of this situation is that there are more single women than single men. In 1970, 68.4 percent of men over 65 were living with a spouse, versus 33.7 percent of women. Another indicator of this female solitude in old age is that widowhood affected only 18 percent of men in contrast to 54.6 percent of women (339). From this arise inevitable human problems, social and others.

Male Fragility is a General Phenomenon

To a considerable extent, male fragility stems from a greater susceptibility to cardiac ailments. Coronary disease is typically a male affair. According to data from the American National Institutes of Health, cardiac ailments kill twice as many men as women (the exact ratio is 1.99). A number of illnesses are even more sexist but less common, and, solely for this reason, are less "androcidal." For various categories of disease, the male-female mortality ratios are as follows (396):

Diseases of the heart: 1.99
Cancer (total): 1.51
Cancer of the respiratory system: 3.43
Cerebrovascular diseases: 1.19
Accidents (total): 2.93
Motor vehicle accidents: 2.90
Other accidents: 2.96
Chronic obstructive pulmonary disease: 2.93
Pneumonia and influenza: 1.77
Diabetes: 1.02
Cirrhosis of the liver: 2.16
Atherosclerosis: 1.32
Suicide: 3.33
Homicide: 3.86
Various causes in infancy: 1.27
All causes: 1.79

In almost all cases, these figures speak for themselves: men pay a higher price to disease than do women. Yet women see doctors more often than do men. This may be in part because women are less reluctant to consult doctors; but it may also be because women are more likely to contract ailments that have little influence on mortality rates, such as rheumatism.

A Female Biological Advantage

These phenomena naturally have diverse causes, such as automobile accidents, which strike many more boys than girls (hence the especially large mortality gap between ages 15 and 24), and alcoholism, which has a predilection for killing men between the ages of 45 and 50.

But these explanations are not entirely satisfactory, for the conditions of life are tending in general toward equalization. Like men, women work, participate in social and political life, drive automobiles, etc. Yet while the risk factors would appear to be in the process of equalization, the mortality gap continues to grow. Thus, a different explanation is called for.

Immunologists appear to be in the process of supplying such an explanation, at least in part. The point of departure for their investigations is the well-established fact that men and women do not display the same level of resistance to a variety of fatal diseases. This was demonstrated as early as 1976 by three French researchers, S. Kerbaum, L. Tazi, and D. Champagne. They were also able to show that this lesser male resistance could not be fully explained by socio-economic factors, such as professional activity, hunting accidents, and war. "This male fragility," they point out, "appears as of birth and is found in animal species whose habits do not endanger the male more than the female. A constitutional factor must therefore be involved" (184). But what could the factor be?

After reviewing the evidence in this area, two researchers at the University of Massachusetts, David Purtilo and John Sullivan, proposed the following hypothesis: "Evolutionary selection has equipped females with X-linked immunoregulatory genes for coping with many life-threatening illnesses." (283) And, in point of fact, men suffer more respiratory infections caused by viruses, more central nervous system infections accompanied by poliomyelitis, more gastroenteritis caused by rotavirus, etc. The virus of viral hepatitis is also found more often in men, whereas the antibodies that confer resistance to it are found more often in women. Nobel Prize winner Samuel Blumberg explains this singularity by an immunological affinity between the hepatitis virus and the sperm cells capable of producing boys (those that carry the male chromosome). By the same token, men would be less well-defended immunologically against the hepatitis virus. Hence the inevitable result: they have fewer of the antibodies that confer resistance to the virus and more of the viruses.

Let us add to all this that the unfortunate male sex, which thus appears really and truly as the weaker sex, must fear not only viruses and bacteria but cancer as well. Thus, men are far more susceptible than women to leukemia. In this case too, a weaker immunological response seems to be involved.

However, Purtilo and Sullivan also assert that "the immunological advantage of females is a two-edged sword" (283). Like every biological phenomenon, it has its downside. Women are more susceptible than men to auto-immune diseases, which are excesses of immunological response in which the organism's defenses turn on the organism itself. Thus, one disease of this type, erythematic lupus, afflicts women nine times as often as it does men. This is also the case for other ailments of the same group, such as Basedow's disease, thyroiditis, and myasthenia.

Genetic Factors are Involved

To support their hypothesis of an immunological difference between the sexes, Purtilo and Sullivan do not rely on studies of the frequency of diseases alone. In that case, their argument would indeed be a speculative one. Instead, their case rests primarily on basic research which strongly suggests that certain genes involved in immune system regulation are located on the X chromosome. Women have a double dose of this chromosome; that is, they have two X chromosomes (men having one X chromosome and another chromosome of a type called Y). Thanks to this arrangement, women may enjoy superior protection from disease. This is a justified biological advantage if one considers, with Purtilo and Sullivan, that women must carry the precious product of conception and must therefore defend themselves for two. The existence of five types of immune deficiency that are found only in men supports this hypothesis. Purtilo and Sullivan's explanation thus rests on a solid basis. Consequently, it is plausible that women's greater longevity is caused at least in part by an immunological advantage of genetic origin.

Other evidence also suggests that genetic factors are involved in differences in longevity. As far back as 40 years ago, Hamilton drew up a list of differential mortality by sex in 70 animal species, ranging from flies to man. The result: in 80 percent of cases, females lived longer than males.

Castration and Longevity

Several experiments in castration also suggest that women may have a greater propensity to increased longevity. Thus, a lifespan of 69.3 years has been recorded for a group of 297 eunuchs, versus 55.7 years for a comparable normal population (143). But there is no call for excessive envy: stricken with debility, the eunuchs in question were living in an institution. Among animals, an average lifespan of 8.1 years has been recorded for castrated cats, versus 5.3 years for non-castrated cats.

These various findings, to be sure, do not add up to definitive arguments. Nevertheless, the existence of a female predisposition to live longer appears substantially to be established. Moreover, gerontological data suggest that, to a considerable degree, longevity is genetically determined. It would therefore be very surprising if the male-female gap in this area reflected no hereditary component.

Is this to say that these matters are fixed for all time? Assuredly not. Here it is worth taking cognizance of an important fact: what is genetically determined may still be subject to modification.

Thus longevity, while it rests on a genetically determined foundation, has been modified in the course of the ages: people live longer today than they did in the past. It is conceivable that this phenomenon is partly due to genetic changes—the healthiest individuals may tend to have the most reproductive success; or, alternatively, marriages between less and less closely related individuals may produce taller offspring and, why not, longer-lived ones. But the main factors involved are undoubtedly cultural and social: progress in hygiene, in medicine, etc. This indicates that it is possible to influence a genetic process.

We should also note, however, that evolution has respected the sexual disequilibrium. Populations are living longer, but the mortality gap between men and women persists. In both cases, progress has produced a favorable outcome, but without eradicating the innate difference, at the very time that non-genetic risk factors have been tending towards equalization (more and more women work, drive, smoke, drink, etc.).

Men May Someday Become the Stronger Sex, Thanks to Aspirin and the Pill

It is not entirely impossible that this difference will disappear someday. The female predisposition to greater longevity necessarily results from certain biological factors that medicine may eventually be able to influence. Indeed, a viewpoint is already emerging here in which the corollaries of masculinity and femininity are expressed in biochemical terms. This presents a three-way advantage: first, it offers a deeper understanding; second, it permits the elimination—even at the price of a certain dryness in language—of any tendency to express oneself in terms of value judgments; and third, it enables one to specify the level at which it is actually possible to act upon nature.

In this regard, the case of cardiovascular disease is of interest. Women possess a clear advantage in this area. But it appears that the pill eliminates this superiority—hence the risk of death by thrombosis among women taking oral contraceptives. Conversely, it appears that the consumption of a small quantity of aspirin on a daily basis may substantially reduce the risk of cardiovascular mortality. In that case, medico-social evolution could lead to an equalization of death rates by the loss of the female advantage and the acquisition of a compensatory mechanism for an innate male weakness. Taking this a step further, one can even imagine the reversal of the existing situation: men may finally become the stronger sex, thanks to aspirin and the pill!

For the moment, this is not the case, and the male sex must content itself with physical advantages of lesser importance: a lower rate of benign illness and greater athletic aptitude.

Sports: Can Women Catch up to Men?

In sports, the ongoing evolution is not without parallels to the evolution in longevity, but in the opposite direction. As with the increase in longevity, records are continually broken for both men and women. Thus the Norwegian woman Grette Waitz succeeded, by running the marathon in 2 hours 25 minutes and 42 seconds, in surpassing Mimoum, the male Olympic champion in 1956—but without approaching the current records of male marathoners.

Can women hope to catch up to men completely? In general, the gap between records for the two sexes is narrowing. For various athletic disciplines, from the 100-meter dash to the 1,500-meter run as well as the 4 x 100 and 4 x 200 relays, the average gap (as a percentage of difference relative to figures recorded in meters–per–second) was 13.98 in 1957 but only 8.94 in 1981 (258). Starting from this point, some people have drawn theoretical curves according to which female champions will soon catch up to their male counterparts—swimmers in 2056, bicyclists in 2011.

In sports, theoretical expectations have barely changed over the last few years—at any rate, not toward a reversal of tendency. Taking into account the evolution of the ten best athletic performances for each sex, Kenneth Dyer predicted in 1980 that equalization for the 100–meter dash would take place in 2071. In 1984, he anticipated it for 2054. For the 200–meter run, according to his 1984 analysis, we must wait until 2066; for the 400–meter, 2020; for the 800–meter, 2021; for the 1,500–meter, 2000; for the 3,000–meter, 2003; and for the marathon, only until 1990 (a prediction that has dramatically failed to materialize).

In reality, these forecasts are based on theoretical assumptions that few experts find credible. Thus, since they start from a lower level, female records have a greater margin for improvement. Furthermore, screening for the best athletes among the female population is becoming more exhaustive, which also tends to reduce the difference in records. But it is hard to see how the difference could be eliminated completely. For in sports, men benefit from greater height (1.73 meters versus 1.64 on average), greater weight (68.5 kilograms versus 64.5), 30 percent more muscle mass, a lower proportion of fat (13 percent versus 24.3 percent, although training can reduce the latter to 15 percent), a larger heart (by 10 to 20 percent), better oxygenation of the blood (by 56 percent on average), a greater quantity of hemoglobin, and of course an absence of pregnancy (55). At the same time, this analysis must be qualified. Certainly these facts imply a female handicap in most areas of athletics. But they also confer certain advantages. Thus, women's higher proportion of fat constitutes a survival advantage in the event of shipwreck. A storehouse of energy, it also facilitates flotation. Moreover, women tend to dominate men in attempts to swim the English Channel: eight of the ten best times on record were achieved by female swimmers. As Craig Sharp has pointed out, it is possible that, as a result of their physiology, women would regularly outperform men in contests involving long-distance swimming followed by races through deserts and mountains (331).

If training can reduce the female handicap, it is clear that it does not eliminate it: with the exception of long-distance swimming, men's records are substantially higher than women's for all sports.

The confirmation without appeal of the male advantage in sports is that one of the usual methods of doping female athletes is to inject them with male hormones. If female athletes were to catch up to male athletes by becoming males themselves, they would merely be proclaiming the superiority of their model. Reaching the heights of performance at the price of negating their sex, they would be unable to contribute to the validation of women.

The sex that is called stronger thus saves its honor on the physical level, thanks to a superiority that is in some ways negligible, in that it does not affect longevity. But conversely, it is important in terms of its capacity to confer status. Here we touch on an essential point. Women's physical advantage, unlike men's, is of no use for success in competition. This is another way of saying that what most concerns the male, in sports as in life, is not success in itself but glory, the possibility of domination.

4

The Two Sexual Strategies

It all begins with one small difference—a difference at the heart of every cell in the body. Our genetic equipment, the genes, are located along twig-like structures, the chromosomes. Each species has a particular genetic array and a specific number of chromosomes. In Homo sapiens, there are 23 pairs of chromosomes, for a total of 46. One pair of the 23 consists of the sex chromosomes, the only chromosomes that differ between man and woman. Man has one sex chromosome of a type called X and another of a type called Y, while woman has two X chromosomes. Each ovum, which contains only half of the maternal genetic stock, thus necessarily contains an X, whereas sperm cells contain either an X or a Y chromosome. Depending on whether it is fertilized by a sperm containing an X or a Y, the ovum will produce a girl or a boy.

Females are the Basic Sex

This is as much as to say that things are determined from the very earliest stage, from the moment when the two sex cells (called gametes) unite to form a new individual, which does not yet exist as a being, but already contains everything in potential.

In the course of the embryo's development, this genetic difference will manifest itself by the expression of one of two blueprints. The fetus initially begins to develop organs of female type. Then, under the influence of testosterone, the male hormone, it masculinizes itself, if it possesses the famous Y chromosome.* Thus, *the male can be regarded as a female transformed by testosterone*. Early castration produces

*Cf. 14, 108, 200, 255, 393, 394.

feminization. As Alfred Jost, a research pioneer in this area, teaches in substance, to become male is a constant struggle. The female sex comes first; it is in a sense the basic sex (23, 176).

Strange to say, the same feminist authors who continually denounce biological approaches to the fact of femininity are easily reconciled to this discovery. They regularly proclaim, and accurately so, that the female sex is the primordial sex, citing as evidence the data of endocrinology and embryology. Clearly, it is possible to denounce a science when it produces unwished-for conclusions, while accommodating oneself to it perfectly when things go in "the right direction."

The Myth of Bisexualism

Another conclusion that is often abusively drawn from embryology is the notion of bisexualism. Because both sexes develop from the same materials, we are asked to believe that they are indistinguishable—that one is simultaneously a man and a woman. This is an illusion, arising from the fact that nature economically uses and re-uses the same materials. The sexologist Gérard Zwang has pertinently commented:

> The human condition is lived only as man or woman. From the moment of fertilization, the die is cast. Some people prate about the bisexualism of every human being. Such a notion does not exceed the scientific level of cocktail-party chatter. . . . The body's sexual heritage cannot be denied. The mannish attitudes of some women and the effeminate attitudes of some men cannot in any way alter their genetic polarity. As for the transsexuals who have their breasts or genitals mutilated or who take hormones in order to grow breasts, they suffer from severe mental illness. (401)

Sexual differentiation leads not only to the formation of the sex organs as such, but also to the formation of other parts of the body that are less directly related to sex, such as the breasts. Thus, sexual development pervades the organism as a whole and not just the organs directly involved in copulation.

A Fundamental Dissymmetry

But let us return to the reproductive organs properly speaking. The male-female difference is visible externally and consists in a dissymmetry: one of the organs is hollow and the other is in relief. From this arises the fact that, among mammals, copulation is a penetration.

This is why, for one partner more than the other, copulation is a conquest, a dissemination, while the other partner places greater emphasis on receptivity and choice. Simone de Beauvoir, for her part, admits as much (and with what insistence):

> Even when she is willing, or provocative, it is unquestionably the male who *takes* the female—she is *taken*. . . . Whether by means of special organs or through superior strength, the male seizes her and holds her in place; he performs the copulatory movements. (30, pp. 23–24)

But the essential dissymmetry is deeper than this. The male is, in the final analysis, the producer of a host of microscopic and mobile cells, the spermatozoa; the female, in contrast, produces relatively large and immobile eggs, at the rate of about one every four weeks (in the human species). The size ratio highlights the immensity of the difference: the ovum is 85,000 times larger than the sperm cell. It is also a rare delicacy—a single one is emitted approximately every 28 days, for a total of around 400 in the course of a woman's life, whereas the male expels around 100 million sperm cells in each ejaculation.

Minuscule missiles, the latter's essential function is to carry the paternal genetic stock to the egg. The egg, for its part, supplies not only the maternal genetic stock, but also nourishment for the little embryo in course of formation.

From the very beginning, this cellular dissymmetry imposes different rules of the game on the partner who, without major investment, can distribute his spermatozoa generously and inseminate multiple females, and the partner who produces a solitary monthly egg and subsequently invests nine months in its development in utero followed by several years of her life (387). *In the first case, the important thing is to spread oneself widely without too much discrimination, in the second, it is to do things as well as possible.* To simplify, let us say that *the male opts for quantity and the female opts for quality.*

The female thus exercises the merit of choice. This has been noted by many scientists, from Charles Darwin to Ernest Mayr and Norbert Bischof. Females exhibit more discrimination than males. There is an abundance of evidence in support of this view. In the course of their parades, males sometimes make mistakes and approach females from closely related species, whereas the latter generally reject such advances (preventing hybridization in those cases where it is possible);

in the absence of females, males may go so far as to parade in front of other males. Nothing similar is observed among females. Another confirmation of this view is that it is almost always the male sex that adorns itself in order to be chosen.*

Seven Essential Differences

Such is the apparent biological origin of the differences in sexual strategy between the two partners. For these differences exist and are in fact very sharply defined. The anthropologist Donald Symons of the University of California at Santa Barbara goes so far as to say, "There is a female human nature and a male human nature" (356). In his controversial but heavily documented book, *The Evolution of Human Sexuality,* Symons argues for the existence of at least seven major differences between men and women in terms of sexuality:

(1) Intrasexual competition generally is much more intense among males than among females, and in preliterate societies competition over women probably is the single most important cause of violence. (2) Men incline to polygyny, whereas women are more malleable in this respect and, depending on the circumstances, may be equally satisfied in polygynous, monogamous, or polyandrous marriages. (3) Almost universally, men experience sexual jealousy of their mates. Women are more malleable in this respect, but in certain circumstances women's experience of sexual jealousy may be characteristically as intense as men's. (4) Men are much more likely to be sexually aroused by the sight of women and the female genitals than women are by the sight of men and the male genitals. Such arousal must be distinguished from arousal produced by the sight of, or the description of, an actual sexual encounter, since male-female differences in the latter may be minimal. (5) Physical characteristics, especially those that correlate with youth, are by far the most important determinants of women's sexual attractiveness. Physical characteristics are somewhat less important determinants of men's sexual attractiveness; political and economic prowess are more important; and youth is relatively unimportant. (6) Much more than women, men are predisposed to desire a variety of sex partners for the sake of variety. (7) Among all peoples, copulation is considered to be essentially a service or favor that women render to men, and not vice versa, regardless of which sex derives or is thought to derive greater pleasure from sexual intercourse. (356, pp. 27–28)

This catalogue obviously includes a number of sexist commonplaces.

---

*This is primarily a theoretical hypothesis. A number of experimental studies more directly support the theory that it is the female who chooses—in particular, that of Malte Andersson on the African widow, a bird species that is well-known thanks to the males' spectacular tail feathers. By artificially elongating the tail feathers of males, Andersson was able to make them more attractive to females and thereby increase their reproductive success (5).

For this reason, it will only be taken into account with reservations. This said, even though it presents the standard masculine ideology, one is in all honesty compelled to admit its accuracy. Take point five: women must be beautiful and men seductive in terms of their success. This is the model commonplace, and one can be sure that women and intellectuals will scornfully reject it in any public gathering. But what is denied in public will as a rule be freely admitted in intimacy. I know no woman who does not agree that a man may be seductive in virtue of his success. Conversely, it is true that a woman may please for reasons other than her beauty alone. But the physical is nonetheless always important.

Proof by Homosexuality

The response to reasoning like Symons's is predictable: to seek exceptions that undercut the rules. What, then, of homosexuals and lesbians? Here are people who belong to one sex yet diverge from the criteria they are expected to follow. The argument is weak: every rule has its exceptions and, obviously, there are always special cases. In this instance, the special cases themselves may reflect biological causes, since homosexuality is at least in part a result of genetic factors.

But in this instance the essential lies elsewhere. In effect, homosexuals only differ from heterosexuals in certain aspects of their behavior. In other regards, they retain specifically masculine behavior. According to Donald Symons, homosexuality actually allows one to observe male and female sexuality in their purest forms. For heterosexuality implies a sort of compromise between the two partners; homosexuality does not.

What does one find? Precisely what Symons's model predicts. For example, the market for homosexual pornography is highly developed. Nothing similar exists for the usage of lesbians. Another significant detail is that there is more homosexual than heterosexual pornography, other things being equal (that is, taking into account the differing proportions of homosexuals and heterosexuals in the population). This accords well with Symons's hypothesis that homosexuality does not present an inverted model of male sexuality but an exacerbated one. Still more significant, specialized establishments, baths, etc. enable homosexuals to engage in multiple anonymous encounters, whereas lesbians typically attempt to weave more lasting ties that involve greater fidelity and affectivity.

Thus, statistics from San Francisco indicate that 25 percent of male homosexuals questioned had had more than 1,000 partners and 75 percent had had more than 100. In contrast, no lesbian had attained the score of 1,000 partners and only 2 percent had had as many as 100.

All this, of course, is accompanied by exceptions, by stable homosexual couples and hyperactive lesbians. Similarly, there are heterosexuals with multiple partners and others in faithful marriages (which, it should be noted, do not necessarily indicate an absence of desire but rather an ethical, cultural or religious choice not to yield to temptation).

Once again, it is not a question of attempting to set up absolute barriers between the sexes, but rather of trying to uncover two distinct types of behavior, two different sexual strategies: one, more male, which consists in a quest for numerous partners and is more concerned with quantity than quality; the other, more female, which seeks to establish deeper ties by making a choice on the basis of more sustained attention.

This point of view, for the rest, contains nothing pejorative to woman. On the contrary, it is she who has the best role, since it is she, rather than man, who is more concerned with quality—unless, of course, one adopts the macho criterion of accumulating superficial conquests. Curiously, this is just what certain feminists have been tempted to do, thus confirming that they are in reality locked into a perspective imposed by masculine values, whereas the whole thrust of the present work is to avoid that trap.

The Female Orgasm: A Useless Vestige?

To the differences in the nature of the relationship sought by the two partners one can add the behaviors of the sex act itself. There is little doubt that, if pleasure is the reward of the act for both partners, it is not necessarily experienced in the same way. In particular, it is clear than man reaches orgasm faster than his partner. Moreover, it is generally he who feels the need to desist first. The British psychiatrist Gleen Wilson—influenced, like Donald Symons, by the modern biological approach, or rather by the sociobiological one—has proposed a simple explanation for this phenomenon: *It is normal for man to take his pleasure more quickly after having inseminated his partner, for if she desisted before male ejaculation had occurred, there would be no chance of reproduction.* Even if the sexes had identical dispositions in this regard, the results would still be poor from the standpoint of natural selection: in 50 percent of cases, women would desist first. One can therefore see why, in the course of evolution, the difference between men and women in this regard must logically have been selected for.

Of course, in this case too cultural factors must be taken into account. Practices of greater or lesser sophistication developed by the two sexes make it possible to improve their performances (21, 121). But the general contrast remains. Furthermore, as Gleen Wilson explains:

> If our chauvinistic society were responsible for female sex difficulties we would expect to observe more reliable female orgasms in primitive societies and subhuman species. Not so. Anthropological evidence indicates that female orgasms are just as elusive in cultures other than our own and they are even more rare in the animal world. (391)

Donald Symons takes this view even further. Noting the irregularity of the female orgasm, he wonders whether it is not ultimately a useless artifact. To be sure, orgasm reinforces female pleasure and so may encourage reproduction. But the factor that limits opportunities for birth is doubtless not a lack of pleasure in woman. It is even possible that the female orgasm dissipates vaginal congestion and encourages the evacuation of sperm. According to Symons, it is thus a sort of vestige deriving from the fact that men and women are built from common materials. Woman would thus, from her kinship with the male, have inherited a useless excitation, a veritable vestigial organ along the lines of the appendix. This is a hypothesis, let us note, that in a sense is purely academic: whatever the origin of the female orgasm may be, what matters for its beneficiaries is to enjoy it, rather than to know whether it comes from a particular embryological residue.

Symons's opinion is contested by Sarah Hrdy, another sociobiologist but one of a more feminist sensibility, who for her part regards woman, and the female primate more generally, as a nymphomaniac. In her view, evolutionist logic leads one to suppose that if the female orgasm exists, it must serve a purpose, as moreover the appendix must too. The fact that an organ has no known function would merely signify that one has failed to discover its purpose, not that it has none (157).

Be that as it may, one thing remains clear: female orgasm is more difficult to attain than male orgasm. As Sarah Hrdy notes, Margaret

Mead spoke of orgasm as a "potentiality," attainable but not achieved by all women (157, p. 166). Female ecstasy, in fact, often involves skillful touches in which many males have no competence.

In contrast, certain monkey specialists claim to be completely expert in this domain. The object of their research is to decide between the two theories that divide biologists, and sociobiologists in particular: namely, is the female orgasm unique to our species, or does it also exist in the animal world? In the first camp one finds Donald Symons but also Richard Alexander, David Barash, Frank Beach, Desmond Morris, Katharine Noonan, and George Pugh; in the second, Sarah Hrdy but also Frances Burton, Suzanne Chevalier-Skolnikoff, Donald Goldfoot, Jane Lancaster, Richard Michael, Elaine Morgan, and Doris Zumpe.

To decide, of course, one had to go look—as Doris Zumpe and Richard Michael did. According to their findings, out of 389 copulations observed in a group of rhesus monkeys, the females in 97 percent of cases showed a clasping reflex, in which they extended their arms toward the male in a spasmodic gesture evoking an orgasm (238). Frances Burton went further by stimulating the clitorises of female rhesus monkeys. She was able to observe signs of an orgasmic phase. Another indicator is that orangutan and chimpanzee females, both in captivity and in nature, may procure themselves pleasure directly by masturbation. It is true that this is observed less often among females than among males. The female orgasm is thus undoubtedly a reality among primates. It remains to discover what purpose it serves. For that, we must broaden our study of the relationship between sexuality and the evolution of species.

5

The Descent of Woman

Woman did not make her appearance in the mid-twentieth century, though the media's emphasis on current events sometimes makes it seem that way. While feminism may not have succeeded in producing in-depth change, it must at least be conceded a certain effectiveness: it has at times created the impression that the female sex did not really exist before the twentieth century—before Simone de Beauvoir and Betty Friedan.

Of course, this reflects an optical illusion. Even without invoking such figures as Flora Tristan (1803-1844), who made herself the champion of a kind of feminism in the early nineteenth century, it must be pointed out that the list of prominent women has been open for centuries, from Cleopatra to Marie Curie, and passing by Irène Joliot-Curie, Colette, George Sand, Virginia Woolf, the Comtesse de Ségur, the Brontë sisters, the Marquise de Sévigné, Olympe de Gouges, Queen Victoria, Catherine the Great, Catherine de' Medici, Ninon de Lenclos, Madame de Pompadour, Héloïse, Eleanor of Aquitaine, Joan of Arc, and even a number of illustrious Gaulish and Roman women: Agrippina, Pauline (the wife of Seneca, who voluntarily followed her husband into death), Eponine, Blandine (martyred at Lyons in the second century), and Victoria.*

From Darwinism to Sociobiology

Not only were women not born with the feminist movement; their origin is much older than history itself. It carries us back to our animal past. Therefore, to understand femininity, we must take a detour through evolutionary theory.

*Cf. 17, 22, 79, 168, 202, 252, 272, 305.

As everyone knows—perhaps especially so since the centennial of Charles Darwin's disappearance was celebrated in 1982—the species were not created all at once. They changed progressively: they have evolved. Darwin's genius was to uncover the essential mechanism of evolution, natural selection. Expressed in modern terms, this is a matter of realizing that random modifications, or mutations, create a certain variety among the genes, from which natural selection chooses. Thus, butterflies whose colors make them difficult to see against the bark of trees may be selected at the expense of other individuals. The color of the species will gradually evolve toward a certain optimal tint, until new factors induce it to adapt in some other way. Just this has been observed among butterflies: in some places, industrialization led to the selection of grayish individuals, whose color provided better camouflage against soot-stained factory walls.

The essential idea of natural selection is thus that *the environment plays a role, not by modifying organisms directly, but by selecting among pre-existent genetic structures.* To be sure, an environmental factor may have a certain effect. For example, sunlight makes it possible to tan. But one must realize, first, that this is only possible if we already have an innate capacity to tan, and second, that only changes affecting our genetic heritage are transmissible and therefore relevant to evolution.

The concept of natural selection has enjoyed a considerable success over the last few years, particularly with regard to the study of the social behavior of animals and humans. Thanks to this Darwinian idea, a new science, sociobiology, has emerged*—extremely controversial at first and at last widely accepted. What is it, exactly? Very simply, sociobiology is the study of the biological basis for social behavior. More specifically, sociobiology studies the behavioral strategies by which living beings can best succeed in genetic terms. Everything takes place as if the chief concern of animals were to discover genetically efficient behaviors. In many cases, this involves trying to reproduce oneself as well as possible—for instance, by having many sex partners. But in other cases, it appears to be more advantageous to assist one's genetic relatives. It must be realized that the evolutionary strategies of living beings vary considerably. Everything depends on the particular situation. For example, one way to achieve the best pos-

*Cf. 2, 19, 20, 27, 69, 86, 212, 213, 389.

sible results is to produce a large number of offspring. Such is the strategy of fish that produce quantities of eggs. Many of the eggs will be devoured, but out of the total, the chances are very good that a few will survive. It is also possible, however, to produce fewer offspring and invest more heavily in each one of them. This is the strategy of man and of primates (the group that includes lemurs, monkeys, and man) more generally. Biologists call the first type of approach "strategy r" and the second type "strategy K."

Male Aggression, the Price of Evolution

From this perspective, the question of sex differences appears in a new light.* The strategy adopted, in terms of behavior, could not be exactly the same for the partner who lays a single monthly egg and the partner who produces a virtually infinite number of sperm. We have already concluded this on genetic grounds alone and, as we saw in the previous chapter, it is confirmed by sociological analysis. But how did events unfold during the evolution of species? Quite naturally the males, whose optimal strategy was to spread themselves widely, paraded to obtain the favors of the females. From this arose the immense and wonderful variety of parade behaviors, from the peacock's tail to the monkey's fanfare and the bellicose confrontations of the musk ox.

Among mammals, males are incontestably more aggressive than females. There are, to be sure, a number of variations from one species to the next, but the general fact is beyond dispute. In the case of the human species, little boys are incontestably more aggressive than little girls. In their now classic work on sex differences, Eleanor Maccoby and Carol N. Jacklin underline this point (216). Out of 94 studies surveyed, only 5 found that girls were more aggressive than boys, against 52 that found the reverse (the remainder found no significant differences). Since Maccoby and Jacklin wrote, most studies in this area have confirmed this tendency. Furthermore, the difference is not only quantitative but qualitative: the forms of aggression vary as well. While boys are as likely to engage in physical as in verbal aggression, girls show an indisputable preference for verbal confrontation (8).

Many other observations confirm the greater aggressiveness of the

*Cf. 32, 47, 66, 132, 221, 332, 338, 344, 387.

male sex. For example, individuals with two male Y chromosomes instead of one, who are called XYY's, commit more violent crimes than normal XY individuals or than carriers of another chromosomal anomaly who have one Y and two X's, who are called XXY's. XXY individuals are also predisposed to marginal behaviors, and are often found in prison as well, but for crimes other than acts of impulsive aggression. Moreover, the role of the Y chromosome as a predisposing factor in aggression, like the role of the male hormone testosterone, appears to be a general fact in the animal world.

Is Evolution a Male Affair?

Though the overall lines of the evolutionist vision are beyond serious dispute, its emphasis on male competition and aggression presents one potential drawback. It may create something of an impression that only members of the reputedly stronger sex engage in competition—that only males evolve. Moreover, in a good many species, is not the female infinitely more drab than the male? Such is the case for pheasants, ducks, lions, etc.

As a first approximation, everything takes place as if evolution were solely a male affair. From this perspective, women would only evolve because they are linked to males.

Oddly enough, the theory of evolution would thereby converge with, or rather readopt, the biblical account of the Creation, in which woman was made from man. Does woman descend from man, or does she descend from the she-monkey in the same sense in which man descends from the monkey? As a result of having studied this question in depth, the feminist sociobiologist Sarah Hrdy believes that she can authoritatively answer the latter question in the affirmative.

Sarah Hrdy is not just anybody. She has made a name for herself (albeit an unpronounceable one) among primate specialists. She has produced authoritative studies on the Hanuman langur to which we shall return in due course. Concurring with a theory already set forth by Darwin, she explains:

> Competition among males is complicated by the predilections of females. Among primates in the wild, female preferences may be critical. Except for humans and an occasional ape, breeding among primates is initiated by the female. (157, p. 24)

Moreover, only men and male orangutans practice rape (157, p. 18).

A Genetic Right of Veto

One rediscovers here the genetic power of woman, already celebrated by the feminist eugenicists at the turn of the century. On this subject, Hrdy's words are evocative: "To each creature, however weak, the option is there to vote, so to speak, with her genes" (157, p. 92). Woman possesses this supreme right over what counts most, namely over life itself. This is an absolute power, but it is also a form of servitude, since it causes females to invest heavily in reproductive activities and prevents them from dispensing with males.

Not only is this role essential, but it does not preclude competition. There are occasions when females dominate males—for example, among lemurs, the least evolved of primates. But more often females engage in competition with one another to keep their males. They vigorously expel outsider females, notably among the marmosets of South America, for whom this phenomenon has been very well described. This is true both for lion-headed and black-faced tamarins and for common and dwarf marmosets. Fights between females are frequent and may be even fiercer than fights between males. In Hrdy's view, "Female intolerance for other breeding females is a major deterrent to male philandering" (157, p. 43).

Female Competitiveness

In a sense, females may be even more competitive than males. As Hrdy explains:

> Whereas males compete for transitory status and transient access to females, it is females who tend to play for more enduring stakes. For many species, female rank is long-lived and can be translated into longstanding benefits for descendants of both sexes. Females should be, if anything, more competitive than males, not less, although the manner in which females compete may be less direct, less boisterous, and hence more difficult to measure. (157, pp. 128–129)

Hence Sarah Hrdy's astonishment: "Here then is the puzzle. Competition between females is documented for every well-studied species of primate save one: our own" (157, p. 129).

But are things quite that obvious? Is it really the case that women engage in few rivalries? That would make singularly little of the quarrels between neighbors or fellow employees and of the subtlety of interactions between women more generally. As Sarah Hrdy writes:

> Consider the problem that a human ethologist would face in an effort to measure quantitatively such phenomena as sisters-in-law vying for a family inheritance which is to be passed on to their respective children, or the competition for status between mothers who perceive, however dimly, that their own "place in society" reflects on the whole family and that it may determine the rank at which their own children enter the community at maturity. The quantitative study of such behavior in a natural setting hardly exists. We are not yet equipped to measure the elaborations upon old themes that our fabulously inventive, and devious, species creates daily. Ethologists who have to contend with malarial swamps and subjects that hide in dense foliage 40 feet above them confront a task simple by comparison. How do you attach a number to calumny? How do you measure a sweetly worded put-down? Until we are able to solve such problems, evidence for this hypothesized competitive component in the nature of women remains anecdotal, intuitively sensed but not confirmed by science. (157, pp. 129–130)

Despite her proclaimed feminism, Sarah Hrdy is not very tender towards women. But that is the price for demonstrating the essential: women are active; they too are competitive creatures, even if they do not manifest competition in the same ways as the male. Clearly, *woman is descended from the she-monkey in the same sense that man is descended from the monkey.*

Infanticide and Sexual Strategies

More than any other scientist, Sarah Hrdy has shed light on infanticide, a fascinating phenomenon that illustrates to what a degree males and females may follow distinct and even opposed strategies. Among the Hanuman langurs of India, dominant males acquire troops of females by driving away the current male leader. They retain his position until they are expelled in turn by a younger and stronger male. When the new leader takes up his position, one of his first concerns is to kill all of the young already born. The sight of these tragic acts has destroyed forever Konrad Lorenz's poetic notion that man is the only animal that kills its own kind. In reality, animals too kill each other within the same species. Why did it take so long to discover this fact? The answer lies partly in the inherent difficulty of observing such events: police officers usually only become aware of a murder upon viewing the body of the victim.

Current evidence suggests that infanticide plays an essential role among primates. In Africa, Thomas Struhsaker has managed to observe two cases of infanticide among redtail monkeys, within a necessarily limited number of hours of observation. For a human parallel, one would have to imagine a policeman witnessing two murders within a single year—in a group of just 70 people.

From a sociobiological perspective, infanticide is a necessity for Hanuman langur males. The female can only reproduce after her infant is weaned. When the infant is killed, she becomes receptive. Installed on his throne for a short period of time, the male has no choice of means.

If the male's genetic interest is clear in this instance, the female's is not. Often she practically accepts this fait accompli. In the tragic universe of the Indian underbrush, the monkeys observed by Sarah Hrdy behave exactly as sociobiological theory predicts. In the case of the little monkey Scratch killed by the male Mug, the grandmother and an old aunt interposed themselves between the infant and the aggressor on each occasion, warding off several attacks. The mother, a very young female, often resisted only weakly. Here is a well-regulated genetic dynamic: the old females, since they were past breeding age, had nothing to lose genetically by defending their infant relative. In contrast, by sacrificing herself, the young mother would have endangered a major reproductive potential. She was better off not taking risks and accepting a new child from Mug. Such is the logic of life. To be sure, it has nothing to do with morality; but nature evokes paradise only for those who know her not.

Why the Male Became a Hunter and the Female a Homebody

The drama of infanticide points to an important question: Why do females tolerate males? Mistresses of the genetic future, one can imagine them accepting copulation but then refusing subsequent contact with the males. Are not the latter also competitors for the use of the surrounding area? The food they consume reduces that available to the females and their children. The reason the females do not reject the males plainly arises from the fact that the male, if he is also the father, becomes a natural ally in the defense of the child—indeed, the best ally possible, because the well-being of his progeny is of paramount genetic interest to him.

This process of alliance has manifestly played a major role in human evolution and in the origin of the behavioral dissymmetry between the sexes that exists today (120). The pre-human female, handicapped by pregnancy and the need to carry her infant, needed the male to bring her food and potentially to defend her (this took place in the savanna, a vast open space where predators can see their prey from far away). The pre-man thus became a hunter and the pre-woman developed the inner world, the hearth, and perhaps also certain cultural practices to increase her chances of survival and those of her children (cf. 360). As a result, today one of the partners is more extroverted than the other, more concerned with the conquest of the outer world.

Is Man Monogamous?

This interpretation of human evolution leads to a question that is more difficult than it seems: Is man monogamous or polygamous? It appears that in around 80 percent of human societies, men have multiple wives. In contrast polyandry, or the multiplicity of husbands, is extremely rare. Monogamous societies are common but in the minority. In a sense, the multiplicity of partners is normal for the male: it corresponds to his sexual strategy as the producer of an infinite number of sperm cells. But on the other hand, an evolutionary sequence encouraging the spread of the nuclear family should lead to monogamy. Moreover, the dissymmetry between many sperm and a few eggs does not preclude monogamy, which in fact is practiced by 37 out of the total of slightly more than 200 primate species.

Strangely enough, although ethnologists and sociologists have long studied this question, it is still not possible to give it an unequivocal answer. There seems to be a certain tendency toward a monogamy accompanied by frequent male infidelities. This may be the best way for the male to win the game: he retains the possibility of multiple genetic investments while preserving himself from the burden of dispersed paternal duties.

Recent work on ape anatomy enables us to understand this problem better without entirely resolving it (340). On one hand, it appears that in monogamous ape species, sexual dimorphism (the apparent difference between the sexes, especially with regard to overall size and the size of the canine teeth) is less pronounced. Thus, male orangutans and gorillas, who possess harems, are much bigger than their female counterparts. From this point of view, human beings are best adapted for monogamy. Men and women differ relatively little in weight and even less in the size of their canines. Another parameter is the size of the testicles. The gorilla and the orangutan, who keep their desired partners with them and need therefore copulate only when useful, have quite small testicles. In their case, selection has favored physical strength over sexual capital. Conversely, the male chimpanzee, who lives in mixed-sex groups and is consequently in permanent sexual competition with his peers, has enormous testicles. In his case, the object is clearly to be able to copulate as frequently as possible. Instead of a larger body than the female, natural selection has equipped him with a high-performance reproductive apparatus.

In this regard, the human male is closer to the gorilla and orangutan—that is, to those animals that find their sexual partners with regularity inside the family structure. But matters grow more complicated with penis size, which is small in monogamous monkeys, larger in the chimpanzee, and much more impressive still in man. All this is somewhat paradoxical; and as, moreover, the tremendous human penis does not appear to be usable as a weapon, it is plausible that its only ultimate purpose is the sexual satisfaction of the female. The latter presents, in terms of particularities, an enormous bosom but an external genital apparatus no larger than that of the female gorilla or orangutan. In this regard, the chimpanzee is unique in having a far larger apparatus, which accords very well with its way of life in societies that practice multimale polygamy and where competition is generalized.

The upshot of all this is that the human species appears to be made for either monogamy or polygamy (with several females to one male), but definitely not for group sexuality.

Is Male-Female Cohabitation a Form of Commensalism?

Clearly, the strategy that oriented our species toward a certain monogamy could only function if the male were also the father of the woman's children. Among primates such as langurs, evolution has selected a different strategy, in which the interests of the two sexes may diverge, and which does indeed lead one to ask why females tolerate males—or more precisely, why selection has not favored females who refuse to reproduce with males inclined to infanticide. Such a policy of boycott was unworkable from an evolutionary standpoint. It would tend to disadvantage the children of females practicing it at the expense of the children of more accommodating mothers. Moreover, the system favors those who cheat. In the event of a boycott, the female who accepts copulation with the infanticidal male wins at every turn: since she is the only one to have any offspring, her genes eliminate all others in a single generation. This type of analysis reveals a nature that is cynical and calculating, a thousand times removed from the beatific visions of some of her contemplators. But what can be done about it?

In this sometimes sordid series of calculations, males and females can have only partly common interests. In a sense, they could be viewed as two different species, each selecting its own strategy, and allying themselves for a common end: the raising of children. In a similar manner, certain fish cohabit with sea anemones. Such cohabitation between two different species with a common interest is called "commensalism." On both sides, it involves calculation and active participation. The female does not follow the male; she accepts him because it is in her interest to do so. Let us say that she accommodates herself to him to her own advantage—which clearly refutes the notion of a submissive and passive female.

Is Nymphomania a Necessity?

The female primate, including woman, may be even more active than is thought—to the point of nymphomania, if one follows Sarah Hrdy:

> An assertive, temporarily insatiable female sexuality, epitomized by the seemingly nymphomaniac solicitations of a Barbary macaque in estrus—what earthly relevance does the conduct of this monkey have for understanding her culture-bearing cousin, whose solicitations are sedate, self-conscious, often elaborate in their subtlety and indirection? (157, p. 160)

Clearly, this primatologist's reply inclines to the affirmative. Moreover, do not statistics suggest a female tendency toward multiple relationships? A 1980 *Cosmopolitan* survey found an infidelity rate of 70 percent among married women over 35. According to the same survey, one in ten women has had more than 25 lovers (cf. 157, pp. 162–163).

Why, from an evolutionary standpoint, should a female have a tendency to seek multiple partners? After all, a single male suffices to

guarantee her a perfect reproductive yield. On the face of it, nymphomania would appear to serve no purpose. This could be called the "theory of saturation," and is strikingly set forth by Donald Symons:

> It is difficult to see how expending time and energy pursuing the will-o'-the-wisp of
> sexual satiation, endlessly and fruitlessly attempting to make a bottomless cup run
> over, could conceivably contribute to a female's reproductive success. On the con-
> trary, insatiability would markedly interfere with the adaptively significant activi-
> ties of food gathering and preparing and child care. Moreover, to the extent that
> insatiability promoted random matings, it would further reduce female reproductive
> success by subverting female choice. (356, p. 89)

To this one can reply that the female, in her quest for quality, has an
interest in extensive trials before making her final choice. From this
perspective, it appears normal that, like the male, she too should enjoy
multiple relations. This qualifies the viewpoint presented in the previous chapter: women, too, may be interested in multiple partners. But
the biological strategy remains appreciably different: in one case, it is
a matter of spreading oneself as widely as possible; in the other, of
making the best choice possible. The female primate has all the more
opportunity to make this choice in that she is only fertile at certain
times. Furthermore, as a general rule, dominant males allow their
females to have adventures during the infertile part of their cycles.
This tendency is clearly visible among monkeys. Among monkeys—
but not among women. For in our species the moment of ovulation is
hidden. Invisible by external signs, it can be detected only through biochemical analysis or, at a minimum, by maintaining charts of body
temperature.

Biologists have propounded a number of imaginative hypotheses to
explain woman's concealed ovulation. For example, Nancy Burley
speculates that, because of his intelligence, Homo sapiens could have
used visible ovulation as a means of contraception (as he in fact has
done through methods of the Ogino type). After all, bearing children is
not without its inconveniences. In the course of human evolution, the
female might have been tempted to enjoy sexual pleasure without
incurring the burdens of motherhood. Evolutionist theory would lead
one to presume that a system which makes it impossible to determine
the time of ovulation must have been positively selected for (156).

Sarah Hrdy, for her part, presents a different hypothesis, which
allows her to connect her two favorite themes, nymphomania and

infanticide. Concealed ovulation would be *the weapon of doubt*. A primate female who has copulated with many males without any one of them knowing for certain whether or not he is the father of her offspring may benefit from multiple collusions. After all, every male who is tempted to kill her young will hesitate if he might thereby be destroying his own progeny. If one admits that the female's reproductive success is largely dependent on the males' tolerance of her young, the hypothesis holds up. Hence Sarah Hrdy's conclusion: "To the extent that her subsequent offspring benefit, the female has benefited from her seeming nymphomania" (157, p. 174).

6

Hierarchy and Gender

Plato first thanked the gods for making him a free man and not a slave, and second for making him a man and not a woman. There could be no clearer statement of the existence of a hierarchical relationship between the sexes. For this reason, to regard males and females as members of two different species living in a state of commensalism, as we have just envisaged from a theoretical point of view, is not only somewhat of a caricature but also imprecise in at least one respect: for males and females interact in a hierarchical fashion.

So far we have mainly invoked competition between males and females. But there also exists, if not a "war between the sexes" (29), then at least a hierarchical relationship between members of the two groups. Moreover, it is in regard to this relationship that the political and social question arises: the male is said to impose excessive tutelage on his companion.

Male dominance is a fact. On this point machos and feminists, sociologists and biologists all agree. As Michelle Zimbalist Rosaldo and Louise Lamphere write:

> Whereas some anthropologists argue that there are, or have been, truly egalitarian societies, and all agree that there are societies in which women have achieved considerable social recognition and power, none has observed a society in which women have publicly recognized power and authority surpassing that of men. Everywhere we find that women are excluded from certain crucial economic or political activities. . . . It seems fair to say then, that all contemporary societies are to some extent male-dominated, and although the degree and expression of female subordination vary greatly, sexual asymmetry is presently a universal fact of human social life. (296, p. 3)

The fact of male dominance is thus beyond reasonable dispute,

49

despite some dated fantasies of matriarchy (287). It is over the origins of this hierarchical relationship that opinions diverge. Some regard male dominance as a fact of nature, others as an artifact tied to certain historical conditions.

One Woman in 600 in a Leadership Position!

In point of fact, women are rarely found in leadership roles. Although increasing numbers of women are entering the professions, it is still rare for them to attain the highest levels in these fields (383). Even when they are present in management positions, they almost never reach the top of the hierarchy (24, 270). A significant detail: the chief obstacle does not appear to be access to entry-level positions but reaching a higher level once such a position is obtained. In this area, the figures speak for themselves. In the United States in 1975, one woman in twenty held a managerial position, but only one in 600 held an executive position. In France, the report on "Women in a Society of Inequalities" has confirmed this tendency for most sectors, and in particular for the field of medicine:

> Although the profession is rapidly becoming feminized (in a few years, more than one-third of doctors will be women), there are *virtually no* women at the top of the hierarchy. This discrimination is also found in the paramedical professions, where many exclusively female branches (midwives) are often hierarchically dependent on men (obstetricians). (203)

When women in numbers do attain a higher position, it often loses its importance; essential decisions are then made at a different level (361). Other things being equal, a man is 80 percent more likely than a woman to be selected for an executive position. Often it is the dominant woman herself who pushes for this decision. She chooses not to be a leader (88).

When they reach the summit of a hierarchy and fail to succeed, women are less apt to be criticized than men. "After all," the primatologist G. Mitchell comments on this subject, "women are not supposed to be good leaders" (243). In general, everything takes place as if the exercise of power were not really women's affair. Moreover—and this point has not been emphasized enough, although it is obvious in daily life—women prefer to be led by men. Nietzsche, among others, observed this very well:

Finally, I ask this question: Has a woman ever recognized any master with a female spirit? And is it not generally the case that it is women who have most despised woman and not we?

The Political Arena

The political arena, where the game of power is played par excellence, appears almost everywhere to be reserved to men. *From the perspective of ethology, female behavior is manifestly less political than male behavior.* Boys between the ages of 3 and 11 already seek attention to augment their power, while girls of the same ages are more likely to ask for help. The former attempt to impose themselves by force, the latter by invoking the rules of the game (385).

All observers have noted women's lesser participation in political life (72)—and that in all countries. In the mid-1950s, Maurice Duverger noted in a United Nations report, *The Political Role of Women,* that the proportion of women in legislative bodies scarcely exceeds 5 percent: 5 to 6 percent in the Netherlands, 5.6 percent in France, 4 percent in Norway, 3 percent in Britain, and 2 percent in the United States. Significantly, the situation does not appear to have evolved in an egalitarian direction since that time. Thus, although 35 female representatives were elected in Japan when women first received the vote there, within a few years this figure had fallen to 11.

Not only do women participate little in political activities, but when they do, they tend overwhelmingly to occupy traditionally female positions. Maurice Duverger's description of this phenomenon is still valid today:

> In party leadership, in senior administrative posts, in parliaments and in governments, the few women included concentrate on specialized matters, such as health, education, motherhood, family welfare, housing, etc.—that is, on all problems which, in the general opinion, are considered to be of special interest to women. (94, pp. 123–124)

Although several cabinet positions have been accorded to women in recent years, one must acknowledge that the tendency described by Duverger persists. With few exceptions, women holding cabinet rank are concerned with feminine activities. Apparently, it does not occur to any president to name them prime minister, minister of the interior, of defense, of foreign affairs, etc.

One striking detail is that those political parties that accord women the most public importance tend to be those that the female sex favors least. For example, the French Communist Party has granted a relatively large number of official positions to women, yet it receives proportionately the lowest number of female votes of any major party. As for women's right to vote, it was more the result of wars and the desire of some male politicians to acquire female votes than of the campaigns of the suffragettes. All of this tends to underscore the female sex's relative lack of interest in political life.

This sociological fact has been virtually untouched by feminist demands. For years, a whole literature of engagement has exhorted women to militancy.* But the success of this appeal has been marginal. Moreover—and this is a major handicap for every form of militant feminism—female politicization runs up against the fact that women do not really regard themselves as a group. As the historian William L. O'Neill writes:

> Women everywhere seem to identify more with their families than with their sex and join men in supporting role definitions that keep women out of politics. This lack of solidarity distinguishes women from the minorities with which they are often compared. Racial and ethnic groups vote in blocs and support their candidates, giving them a leverage that women politicians do not have.

Hence O'Neill's essential idea:

> Behind the question of why women seldom run for office lies the more far-reaching question of why they do not identify with, and are not loyal to, their own sex. (265, p. 219)

Conversely, political activity in the human male corresponds to the male-male relation characteristic of life in bands. A direct extension of the bond that unites the hunters of a tribe, this relation explains group activities as varied as those of British men's clubs, associations of sports fans, and, to some extent, militant political groups (365).

Monarchy Less Sexist than Democracy!

Women can nevertheless become prestigious leaders. History accords places of honor to a host of queens and regents: Semiramis,

*Cf. 1, 63, 67, 74, 85, 98-100, 125, 126, 127, 149, 175, 178, 180, 197, 239, 241, 289, 299-301, 315, 324.

Isabella the Catholic, Elizabeth I, Catherine the Great, Maria Theresa, Queen Victoria, Blanche of Castille, Catherine and Marie de' Medici, Anne of Austria, etc. In France, one should not overlook various revolutionary figures such as the Duchesse de Longueville and La Grande Mademoiselle under the Fronde, Madame Roland, Théroigne de Méricourt, and Olympe de Gouges under the Revolution, Louise Michel under the Commune, and various leaders of contemporary extreme-left movements such as Huguette Bouchardeau and Arlette Laguillier.

A remarkable fact is that, with rare exceptions like Margaret Thatcher, more women have been monarchs, a position inherited from inside the family, than democratically elected leaders. (This also applies to Eva Perón, Indira Gandhi, and Benazir Bhutto.) Can this fact be explained by the less political, because less competitive, character of aristocratic societies in comparison to democratic ones? One thing, at any rate, is certain: in general, only a mitigation of competition (through automatic heredity) allows women to attain the highest ranks of political leadership. Moreover, when they do attain such positions, their presence does not affect the positions' masculine tenor. Israelis liked to say that Golda Meir was really a man, while in France one customarily describes a female cabinet minister as "the only man in the government." It is striking that one of the surest ways for a woman to acquire high political office is to succeed her deceased husband. Many are the wives and widows of mayors, legislators, and still more influential men who have succeeded their spouses, such as Corazon Aquino and Violeta Chamorro. A similar phenomenon is found in all societies. Thus in India, tradition demanded that a Mahrarri princess lead her troops into battle if her husband had died and she had no son (13).

All this, of course, can be explained in a variety of ways—for example, by the fact that the abilities of a leader's wife are more likely to come to public attention. But how can we fail to notice that a wife's acquisition of her husband's rank corresponds to a well-known ethological phenomenon in the animal world? Among many vertebrate species, a female automatically acquires the same rank as her male. It therefore seems plausible that widows constitute, not a representation of their own influence, but a symbol of their husbands'. As Lionel Tiger writes:

Perhaps females possess the "releaser" which stimulates people to follow them mainly when they embody or share the "charisma" of dominance of a closely related male. Otherwise they neither inspire the confidence nor channel the energies of potential supporters.

Thus, that females only rarely dominate authority structures may reflect females' underlying inability—at the ethological level of "pattern-releasing" behavior—to affect the behavior of subordinates. However, this general handicap apparently can be overcome by those females who have obviously participated in the use of power through their closely related men. More than any other factor, this appears to lend efficaciousness to females' otherwise ineffective political efforts. Of course, this is similar to the general process of transmission of charisma from one person to another which occurs in the development of dynastic political traditions. A retired incumbent's endorsement of an aspiring candidate is part of the same process of transmission. Female succession is only one factor in the complex process of maintaining social order. (365, p. 74)

Is the Struggle for Power Women's Affair?

Many hypotheses have been advanced to explain the general character of male dominance: the role of socialization, childrearing practices, etc. All these environmentalist theories doubtless contain an element of truth, but they tend to mistake effects for causes. For they typically ignore the essential: namely, that man's domination of woman is a general fact, which is not restricted to the political sphere and is found in all human societies.

A great deal has been written about this dominance relationship,* explaining in particular that it may arise from a physical superiority enabling men to rule, capture, and rape women (57). This argument has received varying interpretations. It can as well be used to confirm the biological naturalness of sex differences as to emphasize that woman's inferiority is not due to weaker innate abilities but to male tutelage, implying that to cast off this tutelage would suffice to bring about equality at last. Most feminist theorists espouse the latter interpretation. This interpretation nevertheless amounts to admitting that men and women differ in at least one way, namely, in their respective physical aptitudes for domination. Although this interpretation poses no problem for the perspective that is called sexist, which regards men and women as fundamentally different, it is humiliating for the weaker sex from the feminist standpoint. In effect, the first point of view rejects the notion of superiority in favor of the concept of a general difference, whereas the second amounts to regarding woman as equal to man in all ways but one—that is to say, slightly inferior overall, in con-

*Cf. 123, 134, 287, 320, 390.

trast to a stronger sex that is regarded as the model to imitate (391).

In reality, one must ask whether, in this case too, the sexism-feminism dichotomy is not ill-founded, and whether we should not dispense with its reductionism. It is possible that woman's tutelage is primarily a result not of weakness but of a lack of interest in power struggles: that this form of competition is not women's affair. For what one discerns behind professional and political battles for access to power is a certain mode of apprehending the world based on aggression, violence, and virility. But is this women's concern? That is not clear. Moreover, psychopolitical analysis confirms that women's opinions tend to reject anything that leads to violence. Precisely this has been noted not only by psychologists and ethologists but by sociologists as well. As Gaston Bouthoul, a specialist in the sociology of war, observes:

> Even in our day, the principal political problems, namely, questions of foreign policy, continue to be posed in scarcely-veiled terms of war and violence. By temperament and by the logic peculiar to them, women can neither acknowledge nor understand these questions. War remains the great affair of men. Man appears to be organically incapable of answering the question, "If we do not make war, what will we do?" (51, p. 52)

If one follows the politicological conception of Carl Schmitt, it would thus appear entirely normal that men, who alone accept war—that is to say, the ultimate extreme of the distinction between friend and foe—should be the only ones to truly engage in politics (72).

Testosterone: the Power Hormone?

For the biologist, observation of the male-female difference in regard to power-seeking points to an obvious working hypothesis: could a hormonal factor be involved? A number of authors have raised this possibility. For example, according to J. Dearden, testosterone confers greater aggressivity (87). Studies of apes confirm this assertion: hierarchical position in a group correlates with testosterone level (297). As it happens, this relationship involves an element of circularity: a certain level of testosterone facilitates access to power, and hierarchical success in turn reinforces the biological process by raising testosterone levels still higher.

Woman, less oriented toward the spirit of conquest, is more concerned with herself and her home, while man is more concerned with directing his activity toward the outer world. A fact in line with everyday experience is that women are more interested in the local aspects of political life, while men are more interested in problems of wider geographical scope. The Canadian anthropologist Roger Larsen presents a similar point of view when he says:

> Men tend to occupy the roles that are socially defined as the most prestigious, even if they are not the most admirable. . . . Men tend to occupy the most physically aggressive and politically active positions. There are exceptions to this: some women have adopted the "executive" role, though without changing its masculine definition. Like all exceptions, they are remarkable for their statistical insignificance and their idiosyncrasy. Culture and testosterone appear to be in remarkable agreement over the roles of men in social groups. (195, p. 353)

7

The Pirandello Effect

You can perform the experiment yourself. Take a baby young enough that its sex is not visible and present it to people who have never seen it before. To some, you say it is called Mary; to others, John. How do they find it? For sure Mary will be cute, flirtatious, sweet, and charming, while John will be big, strong, mischievous, and daring.

Plainly, people tend to feminize girls and masculinize boys. Customary in our species, this tendency to label—which extends to many things other than the male-female relationship—leads parents to react in more or less stereotyped ways to their children's sex. Girls will be taught gentleness and how to impose themselves through charm, while boys will be taught a certain sense of masculine competitiveness ("If your classmate is hitting you, you have to stand up to him"). And to prevent any ambiguity, clothing will serve as a genuine uniform.*

At this point, the question arises: are masculinity and femininity purely the result of such labeling? Are they something artificial imposed by a sexist upbringing? And, if so, shouldn't we expect that the more egalitarian childrearing practices in vogue for the last few years, along with the unisex fashions that often accompany them, will render obsolete the traditional images of the little boy and little girl? Certainly, many writers have taken this position—Elizabeth Badinter, for example, who perfectly summarizes the prevailing view in a few lines:

> When one views them from behind or from far away, with the same clothes and hairstyles, the young man and young woman tend to merge: less bust, less hips and

*On femininity and masculinity, see 18, 264, 280, 294, 345, 362, 380, 388.

thighs among the women; less muscle and shoulders among the men. Unisexism exists, at least in appearance.

From the psychological point of view, it is difficult today to say what distinguishes the little boy from the little girl. . . . Nothing shows that passivity is exclusive to girls, any more than suggestibility or a tendency to underrate oneself. Nor does anything show that competitiveness is more common among boys, or fear, timidity, and anxiety among girls; that boys have dominating tendencies and that girls have a greater capacity for submission; or even that so-called "maternal" and "nurturing" behaviors are more specifically female than male. (16, p. 370)

The Little Boy: A Born Macho?

Then is gender identity an artifact, soon to disappear under the influence of new fashions? Clearly, to approach this question in a scientific manner, one must divest oneself of the received notions of everyday conversation and refuse to rest content with simplistic experiments. On the contrary: we must look elsewhere altogether, at the very origin of the difference—for example, at childhood, when gender identity is forged; at primitive societies where the burden of sexism differs from that prevailing in Western lands; and above all, at biological exceptions in which gender identity changes.

For the child, things quickly become clear: playing soldier or cowboy is male, as is playing with cars. Conversely, playing with dolls is female. There is also a noticeable sexual dissymmetry: while girls do not mind playing boys' games, boys despise the ways of the other sex. As a general rule, boys view effeminacy, especially in a member of their own sex, as grounds for derision. Plainly, they regard everything belonging to the female sex as inferior (399). Their whole attitude and even their jokes bear witness to this. Is it any wonder, then, if so many of them grow up to be machos?

What is the source of this initial difference? This question is difficult to answer on an a priori basis. The precocious character of the difference suggests a degree of predisposition. But if one views the child as an especially malleable being on whom familial influences operate continuously, one can equally well see nothing in it but the first signs of conditioning to sexism. However, there are still grounds for believing that the little male contains some innate propensity toward machismo: for if this were not the case, how could one explain why everything always evolves in the same direction!

From the Kalahari to the Kibbutz:
The Triumph of Human Nature over Culture

To resolve the issue, one extremely desirable approach would be to examine primitive societies that are less sexist than our own, such as the Bushmen of the Kalahari Desert. Among the Bushmen, parents apparently make no attempt to influence their children's development in either masculine or feminine directions. The Bushmen thus constitute a nonsexist society in this respect. Despite these entirely favorable conditions, the ethnologist Patricia Draper has found that the girls spontaneously engage in feminine activities; the boys, in masculine ones. The boys venture further from the group, whereas the girls exhibit greater caution (93). These observations, which are confirmed by other studies (46), invite us to cease regarding the differences between boys and girls as unimportant.

Indeed, they are so important that societies dedicated to the realization of sexual equality have been forced to beat a prudent retreat.

Consider the case of the Israeli kibbutzim. During the 1940s and 50s, these cells of collectivist life proclaimed themselves as a break with the intensely patriarchal character of Jewish life. Imbued with the ideologies of socialism and egalitarianism, the kibbutz members sought to apportion all tasks equally, regardless of sex. Distinct roles for men and women were to be eliminated. Amid the enthusiasm proper to pioneers, everything seemed to be going well at first. Then the women revealed themselves to be less interested in politics and leadership positions, abandoning these activities to the men. More concerned with their households, they broke with the ideology of the kibbutz and demanded more time with their children. Still more striking, this process accelerated among the daughters of the pioneering generation. The women of the second and third generations insisted that they be allowed to spend even more time with their children, and some deliberately refused top management positions when these were offered to them. This was the end of the egalitarian experiment in the kibbutz (366). In his book *Gender and Culture,* the anthropologist Melford E. Spiro recounts the erosion of this ideal (76, 347). He describes the cycle of events involved as "the feminist revolution and the feminine counterrevolution" (347, p. 79). Thenceforth, different tasks were assigned to men and women: to men, the high-status occupations; to women, the supervision and care of the children. It was, in Spiro's words, "the triumph of nature over culture" (347, p. 100). More precisely, it was the triumph of reality over fantasy.

Proof by Transsexuality

As striking as these findings are, they do not, of course, amount to conclusive demonstrations. The real proof may have been supplied by the extraordinary observations of Julianne Imperato-McGinley of Cornell Medical School. Imperato-McGinley studied 38 men in Santo Domingo with a peculiar ailment: their hormonal systems do not allow the formation of male genital organs at the time of birth. After having been little girls, they become boys at the onset of puberty. Their testicles descend, their clitorises become penises, and they change sex.

Up to this point, they have been reared as girls. But despite this social identification with the female sex, once they become boys they proceed to assume male identity with little or no difficulty. It is as if the socialization to femininity were ineffectual compared to the power of hormones (163, 164, 377). Moreover, this finding is not unique to Santo Domingo. Parallel cases exist elsewhere; but in Western countries, surgeons usually intervene to conserve the initial sex, which is wrongly judged to be the appropriate one. Nevertheless, reports Julianne Imperato-McGinley, a number of untreated disorders of this type are known in France, England, and Italy—with the same psychosocial consequences as those observed in Santo Domingo.

Dr. Robert Goy of the University of Kansas has provided experimental confirmation of these conclusions by injecting female rhesus monkeys with male hormones. These animals subsequently behaved like males. Goy concludes that "these animals behave like boys because of the masculinizing hormones, not because of a male appearance that causes the other animals to treat them like boys" (377).

Twenty-five Years of Research to Discover What Every Mother Has Always Known

Oddly enough, the first scientific work in this domain tended to point in the opposite direction. Among the many pioneering findings of John Money,* one of the most frequently cited was that concerning children

*Cf. 103, 226, 247, 248.

whose sex had been "reassigned" and who subsequently assumed the sex to which they had been assigned. A parallel case involved a twin boy whose botched circumcision required amputation of the penis: he was transformed into a girl and subsequently behaved like one.

This is known as the "Pirandello effect," in which a child becomes what he is asked to become (214). To be sure, this occurred over twenty years ago, at a time when the child was generally regarded as a malleable being. A "Pygmalion effect" was also described, in which a child becomes what a schoolteacher makes of him. The Pygmalion effect's reputation was short-lived. It was soon undermined by the further development of psychological research. Since that time, proofs of the importance of biological determinism have been steadily accumulating. The fact that gender identity or experience can be changed by a surgical operation or by injections of hormones can no longer pass for proof of the absence of genetic determinism—quite the contrary. The genes do not operate by diffuse influences but by coding for specific chemical syntheses. In substituting himself through drugs for the organism's innate chemical processes, the doctor merely mimics a natural process. He has, in reality, done anything *but* demonstrate that such a process does not exist.

Thus, after 25 years of arduous research, it is now possible to affirm, against the majority of "philosophers," that little boys and little girls are different. To be sure, every mother on earth had always known as much.

Perhaps Gender Identity is Beneficial!

It is now established beyond reasonable dispute that biological predispositions make an essential contribution to the more or less masculine or feminine character of the individual. But must one therefore conclude that society's labeling has no effect? I would find that very difficult to believe. Furthermore, in my view the question is badly formulated. The usual approach is to ask whether an observed sex difference is cultural or biological in origin, as if these were two unrelated factors exercising their effects in opposite directions. The prevailing equation is: either sex differences do not exist, or if they do, they are caused by cultural factors despite innate equality; or else biological differences are responsible, in which case cultural factors can be ignored.

In my view, once the existence of biological determinism is

acknowledged, the problem can no longer be stated in this way. For if sex differences exist, even relatively minor ones, and if they arise from a biological imperative, then it is normal for society and culture to take them into consideration and potentially to amplify them. For instance clothes, which are certainly cultural creations, are also and perhaps primarily biological necessities. They serve to protect us from the cold. They also serve to indicate membership in a group (military, ecclesiastical, etc.) and hierarchical status. But these are only ways to reinforce biological necessities that are partly concealed in our species. Just as we no longer have fur to protect us from the cold, we lack erectile hairs or crests to indicate our social standing. In place of fur and other natural characteristics, clothing fills these functions; it complements the biological rather than replacing it. It exacerbates a tendency but does not create that tendency. In my view, the same situation prevails in the development of gender identity. The differentiating practices of child-drearing do not create the initial difference, but they exacerbate it; they assist every individual to reinforce his or her identity.

This brings us to an important question. The feminists—and this is one of their principal quarrels with psychoanalysis (241)—typically see nothing in gender identity but a destructive social institution, since it is a factor in sexism. But what if gender identity were also and perhaps primarily a beneficial process that helps everyone to feel at ease with and take charge of himself? Norbert Bischof, director of the department of mathematical and experimental psychology at the University of Zurich, states this point with exceptional clarity:

> One may well wonder whether boys would become happy adults if, from early childhood on, their natural tendency toward competition were saddled with a guilty conscience. And, similarly, whether girls would grow up to be happy women if they were subjected to social pressures requiring them to behave like tomboys. (40, p. 49)

But it is not simply a question of seeking happiness. For the human condition is lived as something: as man or woman, child or adult, black or white, athlete or intellectual, liberal or conservative, etc. To be sure, the labels we give each other are often naive and sometimes artificial. But bisexualism, apoliticism, everything that translates into non-belonging, non-involvement, and absence of choice is only a way to flee the human condition. Such is, moreover, the fundamental problem with 1960s-style feminism. On one hand, it seeks to impose femininity as the only ultimate value; on the other hand, it rejects the existence of "the Eternal Feminine." On one hand, the feminists seek to rediscover a female nature supposedly denied and alienated by centuries of male oppression; on the other hand, they reject this nature as a myth created by sexism.

8

Sex Differences in Brain Structure

There are times when everyone agrees to assert a position while secretly believing the opposite. This strange sort of consensus makes it possible to avoid a potentially disagreeable argument while more or less unconsciously keeping sight of one's bearings. The question of female psychology clearly reflects such a consensus. Everyone secretly believes that men and women think in very different ways, but no one (at least in intellectual circles) dares to take any position other than the absolute sameness of the sexes in this area.

This ideological burden may turn out to have been a blessing in disguise. A veritable challenge, it has forced scholars to probe deeper, to advance to a more fundamental level of analysis. If the question of sex differences involved psychology alone, it might indeed be difficult to understand clearly. Researchers would consider it frivolous and, frankly, would not dare to study it. But in recent years, the debate has shifted to the fields of brain anatomy, neurochemistry, and endocrinology. Here, on the face of it at least, there should be greater scope for objectivity.

The Death of a Dogma

Until just a few years ago, the only thing known for certain in this domain was that women's brains are somewhat lighter than men's; but their total body weight is also lower. The generally accepted conclusion was still that formulated by F.P. Mall in 1909: every scientific attempt to discover a sex difference in the brain had failed. Nothing much, then, to add to the file.

However, in the last few years an avalanche of findings has demonstrated the existence of such differences. In the first place, there are

65

numerous studies of animals, particularly birds. The canary is an especially good example. Fernando Nottebohm has demonstrated the existence in the male of a mass of cells that are infinitely more developed than in the female. Moreover, this mass is located in the noblest part of the brain, the frontal lobes. This physiological characteristic is directly involved in song—hence its development in the male. In this instance, a difference in form clearly corresponds to a difference in function.

But birds are not mammals and what one observes in their brains cannot be applied directly to our own species.

More interesting, therefore, are studies of monkeys and rats. In these animals, sex differences have been detected in several parts of the brain—for example, in the hypothalamus, the command center for many activities and notably for sexual behavior; and in the amygdala, a part of the brain located above each ear that may be involved in aggressive behaviors. A coherent picture uniting physiological and behavioral data is beginning to emerge. It has even been shown that there are more cells in certain parts of the brain in one sex than in the other, or, moreover, that they are organized differently.

What about man? Dissection cannot be practiced as readily as with rats in this case. Nevertheless, many autopsies have been performed. They confirm the existence of certain anatomical differences. In 1983, Christine de Lacoste-Utamsing of Columbia University demonstrated that the corpus callosum, which links the two halves of the brain, is considerably larger in women than in men (192).

Since this initial discovery, several neurophysiologists have confirmed the existence of sex differences in the human brain. Very recently, two Dutch researchers, D.F. Swaab and E. Fliers (355), have managed to demonstrate a difference in the number of cells of a small part of the brain (the preoptic area of the hypothalamus). All these findings are of course the subject of further research and, on various points of detail, they do not elicit unanimity. But one thing, in any event, has been firmly established: *sex differences do indeed exist in the human brain,* and even in metabolism, to judge by the variations in blood flow that have recently been observed (141). To pronounce on the significance of these differences is, of course, another matter.

Differences Visible to the Naked Eye

The discoveries already reported are so fully confirmed that they appear obvious today. "It is ironic," says Bruce McEwen, one of the leading specialists in this field, "that these studies went from the most complicated and laborious technique and then became progressively simpler"—to the point that the sex differences in the corpus callosum and the preoptic area of the hypothalamus are actually visible to the naked eye.

"Maybe," continues McEwen, "people were afraid to look and didn't believe they could see anything" (189).

While the neuroanatomists were finally seeing what they had been afraid to look for, their colleagues specializing in hormones were also making interesting discoveries. To begin with, they were able to confirm that the brain is indeed the regulator of hormonal activity. It was already known that the glands chiefly responsible for hormone production (the sex glands, the adrenal glands, the thyroid, etc.) are largely regulated by a master gland at the base of the brain, the pituitary. Two Nobel Prize winners, Andrew Schally and Roger Guillemin, were able to demonstrate that the pituitary is in turn controlled by another part of the brain, the hypothalamus.

As the regulator of hormonal activity, the brain is also the director of sexual activity. But—and here we touch on a still more recent set of discoveries—if the brain intervenes in sexual activity, it is itself influenced by sex hormones. Sex hormones interact with the brain; they possess special receptors on the nerve cell membranes.* From here to the thought that, in the course of our development, the most precious of our organs is permeated with the very substances that define gender, is just a short step, which experience invites us to take.

A coherent picture progressively emerges: physiological differences in the brain exist and *the brain is influenced by sex as much as it influences sexuality* (91). This confirms an old intuition that was previously more mythic than scientific, the one that unites sexuality and thought. This is good news for the neuroendocrinologist Roger Gorski of the University of California at Los Angeles, who exclaims enthusiastically: "I've always said that the brain was a sex organ!"

In Woman: A Less Asymmetrical Brain

From here, is it possible to carry the biological explanation further?

That is the whole question, for, as the psychologist Arthur Arnold says, "The question is no longer even whether there are differences in

---

*Cf. 7, 11, 12, 53, 137, 146, 191, 218, 229-231, 259, 260, 275, 285, 310.

nervous organization between the sexes, but rather to understand the sequence of events that explains the differences observed." In short, the differences are an established fact. All that remains is to explain them and specify their significance. This is particularly the case for the differences in cerebral asymmetry.

It has long been known that the two hemispheres of the brain, despite their apparent similarity, do not fulfill exactly the same functions. Thus, in most people, the left hemisphere plays an essential role in speech. It is said to dominate the right hemisphere. Until recently, this dominance was thought to be comprehensive. In reality, the right hemisphere is more important in certain activities. It now appears that this cerebral asymmetry, which has long fascinated neurophysiologists, is more pronounced in males than in females.* Here the meaning of Christine de Lacoste-Utamsing's discovery becomes clear: if the corpus callosum, which connects the two hemispheres, is so highly developed in woman, it is perhaps because the two sides of the female brain are more intensively interconnected.

Difficulty Separating Intellect and Emotion

From the discoveries regarding cerebral asymmetry flow numerous consequences in the area of psychology. The right side of the brain appears to be more involved than the left side in emotional life. Woman, having a less asymmetrical brain than man, may have, as a highly regarded specialist, Sandra Witelson of McMasters University in Hamilton, Ontario says, "a bi-hemispherical representation of emotion."

"If that is the case," continues this psychologist, "it could have major implications in daily life. Women, as a result of such a neurological organization, would be less able to dissociate their emotional behavior from verbal analysis" (397, p. 298).

When it was described in the newspaper *Le Monde* by Dr. Escoffier-Lambiotte (112), this theory unleashed a flood of angry letters from scandalized readers. The theory, to be sure, still lacks concrete confirmation outside of its theoretical justification and—it must be said—the experiences of daily life. Sandra Witelson herself refers to these: "Ordinary observation, in non-experimental conditions, suggests that

*Cf. 165, 166, 174, 205, 206, 233, 370, 397.

women are less able to compartmentalize their emotional responses from their rational analytic behavior. This position is supported, for example, by the effect of emotional stress on the work capacity of men and women." At the same time, it is important not to read too much into these hypotheses, for as Witelson notes: "This difference does not make one sex superior to the other. Different advantages may be associated with the integration of emotion in the rational process and with the independence of both processes" (397, p. 298).

The Same Level of General Intelligence Despite Undeniable Differences

Biology also encounters psychology.* In this domain, research has been underway for many years. Numerous studies have compared the intelligence of women and men. Intelligence quotients (IQ), as well as general evaluations of intelligence, show no significant differences (although IQ tests are designed to minimize any sex differences in scores). But can it be said that the forms of intelligence are the same? Assuredly not.

While noting that IQ's are similar between the sexes, as highly reputed a specialist as Jarvik has not hesitated to write, "with the information now in hand, it is as unrealistic to deny the existence of intellectual differences between the sexes as it would be to negate their physical dissimilarities" (171). The principal difference involves spatial aptitudes, which make it possible to visualize a three-dimensional object in space, to rotate it mentally, etc. Almost all studies, in all cultural contexts, with the possible exception of the Eskimos, have confirmed this difference.** This fact is so well established that it has elicited numerous hypotheses linking certain aspects of intelligence to the sex chromosomes (42, 50, 364).

One of the most attractive of these theories is that of Bock and Kolakowski (48). In order to understand their hypothesis, it is necessary to bear in mind that we have a double set of chromosomes—that is, each gene is paired with a homologous gene, the two together being called alleles. The exception to this rule, of course, is the sex chromosomes in the male, who has one X and one Y chromosome. When the

*Cf. 89, 92, 107, 113, 153, 155, 162, 171, 172, 173, 177, 187, 228, 234, 245, 246, 253, 266, 269, 279, 281, 295, 328, 329, 330, 333, 336, 341, 343, 372, 381, 386, 398.
**Cf. 147, 169, 172, 232, 256, 263, 316, 382.

allele genes carry different instructions (for example, when one codes for blue eyes and the other for brown), one of them is able to win out over the other. This gene is said to be dominant and the other gene recessive. Bock and Kolakowski's hypothesis is based on this concept.

If recessive genes are able to help determine a high level of intelligence, they will have twice as many chances to do so in males as in females, since they will always express themselves, not being faced with possible domination by a less favorable gene. Numerous observations support Bock and Kolakowski's model. For example, there is a stronger correlation in spatial aptitude between mother and son (whose sole X chromosome can come only from her) than between mother and daughter (who also carries an X chromosome from her father). There is also the fact that twice as many men as women surpass the average level (which is not to suggest that the more gifted female subjects—those who in this hypothesis carry two good genes, one on each of their X's—would be inferior to their male counterparts). But a number of observations suggest that a more complex model may be necessary: thus, female subjects with Turner's syndrome, who possess a single X and no Y (they are called XO), are not at a higher level than normal women (on the contrary). It must therefore be admitted that the Y chromosome also plays a certain role.

Why Women Assemble Watches but Do Not Repair Them

The male's superior spatial aptitude may be linked to the prehistoric hunter's need to reconnoiter the surrounding area. Natural selection would thus have imposed this ability as a necessity. Here we again encounter the relationship between the data of psychology and those of sociobiology, and we will see later on how all this fits in with discoveries in endocrinology.

Functional in the past, the male spatial aptitude may still have consequences today, particularly in terms of career choice. In this area there are many small facts that are widely neglected but so important in daily life that they have forced at least one sociologist to reconsider her entire analysis of sex differences. As Evelyne Sullerot frankly explains:

> My work in France involves career counselling for adult women. I decided to study the career orientation and training of girls and women in seven European countries, East and West. Ten years ago, when I began this project, I was convinced—and my

publications record this—that social conditioning and education were entirely responsible for all the differences observed between men and women in career choice and career success. I still think this is true for an extremely large part of the differences in interest and taste that help determine one's choice of training and career.

All the same, my environmentalist faith was shaken by facts—by stubborn facts. Hence I have followed the opposite path from those who of late have inordinately magnified the role of social causes. Social analysis no longer seemed sufficient to explain sex distributions in certain occupations, or the failure of certain educational experiments that were meant to change stereotypes. I began to look at the results of the differences in spatial aptitudes between boys and girls. Not, to be sure, that I think they explain everything! I would simply like to state that, starting from facts that have major economic and social consequences for women, I began, of course, by explaining everything in terms of the environment, the interconnectedness and ubiquity of stereotypes, the difficulties facing girls in entering new fields, and the politico-economic domination exercised by men for their selfish benefit.

I investigated individual sectors of precision engineering, such as watchmaking, where the tasks do not call for physical strength and the environment is neither dirty, noisy nor rank with the smell of burning oil. I also knew that women had been involved in jewelry making since the Middle Ages, and watchmaking can in a sense be seen as a branch of jewelry making. I had to face the facts: everywhere, women make clocks and watches, rapidly and expertly. With extremely rare exceptions, they do not design the mechanisms, do not invent any, and do not even repair them. In the Soviet Union, girls and boys were initially placed in the same watchmaking schools. Today, there is one course of training for assembly and another for repair; there are only girls in the first and only boys in the second. This division was not intentional, and was even resisted. Yet little by little it imposed itself. I could give many other examples, all of them involving professions in which spatial aptitudes are a factor. Such differences between girls and boys may be exploited and transmitted by socioeconomic and sociopolitical structures that magnify their effects. These social structures cannot be considered the sole causes of the consequences observed. The structures make use of differences, and resonance phenomena are produced. (351, pp. 281–282)

Girls are Less Gifted at Math

Spatial aptitudes are also closely linked to mathematical ability. It is hard to believe the number of studies, articles, and books that have been devoted to female weakness in this area in the last five years.* The starting point for these investigations is the fact that very few women pursue careers in mathematics. (This is also the case in computer science.**) David Maines recently published a study of mathematicians in the Chicago area. The result: 168 people contacted in three universities and a proportion of only 10 percent female PhDs in

*Cf. 59, 122, 322, 335, 368, 374.
**Cf. 26, 139, 150.

mathematics. This is certainly an eloquent figure, but one that is susceptible to a variety of explanations. And the explanation offered by David Maines is the closest one possible to the dominant ideology: women are subjected to pressures that do not especially encourage them to pursue careers in mathematics.

Most commentators would not have gone beyond this explanation, which caters to the desire for intellectual comfort, if two psychologists at Johns Hopkins University, Camilla Benbow and Julian Stanley, had not conducted more exhaustive research. Their research was conducted first on 10,000 children in the Johns Hopkins area, and subsequently on a sample of 40,000 Americans! As of the publication of the first part of their work, the results were clear: more boys than girls get good grades in math. Better still, or rather worse, as one ascends the hierarchy of mathematical ability, the differences become more and more overwhelming. Faced with increasingly difficult problems, even relatively high-scoring girls fade away. Intelligence tests that examine mathematical aptitude confirm this major gap (34).

On its publication in 1980, Benbow and Stanley's study created something of a furor. To tell the truth, it outraged intellectual opinion.* Yet its appearance in the most prestigious American scientific journal, *Science,* made it difficult not to take it seriously. Three years later, in the same journal, the authors repeated the provocation. But this time, their sample included 40,000 people, and the results were even clearer with regard to differences at the highest levels of ability. Consider SAT (Scholastic Aptitude Test) scores of 420 and higher: the ratio of male to female success is 1.5, meaning there are 15 boys for every 10 girls reaching this level. But at the 700 level, the ratio reaches 13: in other words, in the Johns Hopkins area, 113 boys scored this high in contrast to only 9 girls. Outside the Johns Hopkins area, the respective figures were 147 and 11. After this, is it still possible to speak of chance and cultural influence? Most experts find that difficult to believe.**

---

*Cf. 31, 36, 68, 102, 182, 211, 249, 323, 348, 369.
**The relative female weakness in mathematics should not be considered as an absolute. History has in effect retained the names of several female mathematicians. Already in antiquity, Hypatia, daughter of Theon of Alexandria, devoted herself to mathematics and philosophy. In the seventeenth century, the Italian woman Marie Gaetane Agnesi (1718-1799) was the first female professor of mathematics in a university. In France, Sophie Germain (1776-1831) corresponded with Gauss (under a male pseudonym—*stéréotype oblige!*) and developed a theory of elastic surfaces. In the same period in England, Mary Fairfax Sommerville introduced the celestial mechanics of

More Precocious and Better in School

Girls make up for their inferiority in mathematics with other qualities. There is no doubt that they regularly outperform boys at school in overall achievement, particularly in English, and above all in reading. They are able to articulate sounds like "ba" and "ma" at an earlier age, and form words and sentences sooner. While boys' superiority in spatial aptitudes appears around the age of 10, girls' linguistic superiority appears very early in life, which strongly suggests that this aptitude is largely independent of environmental constraints (334). With age, the difference tends to diminish.

What does not diminish, very often, is the general superiority of schoolgirls over schoolboys: among girls there are fewer dunces and more advanced students. This could be the result, to a considerable degree, of a greater aptitude for study. In an examination of over 2,000 student records, Schmidberger has confirmed this quality—which, moreover, increases with age. There is a 9.4 percent female advantage in subjects that require study in the first year, which grows to 22.3 percent in the second year. Girls are more attentive, more docile with teachers, attend class more regularly, etc. The girls' advantage appears so clearly that, in kindergarten, differences due to sex are at least as great as those due to social class. At the secondary level, distinctions arising from social milieu become more determinative. In addition, at the highest social level, sex distinctions finally blur. Among students overall, 32 percent of boys are considered unstable, versus 6 percent of girls; 19 percent of boys participate genuinely in class, compared to 37 percent of girls; 49 percent of boys participate passively, compared to 57 percent of girls. After four years of schooling, there is already a far larger number of boys than girls held back for a year or more (400). While the girl's good study habits continue for a long time, all the way to the college level, it is no less striking that the number of outstanding female individuals remains limited.

Laplace in her country and educated Ada Byron, countess Lovelace (1815-1891), who collaborated with Charles Babbage, pioneer of computer science. The Russian woman Sonya Kovalevski (1850-1891), a student of Weierstrass, became a professor at the University of Stockholm, thus triumphing over ambient sexism. Closer to our time, the German woman Emmy Noether (1882-1936), a collaborator of David Hilbert and daughter of the mathematician Max Noether, contributed to the development of algebra, despite the impossibility, on account of her sex, of receiving due university recognition.

The Average and the Extremes

Here we touch on an essential question. Whatever else may be said, the average differences between the sexes, even in the case of spatial aptitudes, remain relatively weak. For that matter, at what point is it possible to affirm that a difference is significant? The choice is a matter of appreciation, of a priori, even of prejudice.

If the averages differ little, should it be concluded that there is no social impact? There is an overlap: even when one sex is noticeably more able in a given area, the overlap rules out any notion of absolute superiority or inferiority. Some representatives of the group that is on average less able will perform better than some members of the other group. But conversely, differences in averages, even small ones, can result in major differences in extremes. Several biologists and psychologists have noted this in regard to intelligence: even a slight shift in the distribution curve of intelligence quotients would have vast social consequences, for the number of exceptional individuals (those who make society advance) could be multiplied by a major factor.

With regard to the comparative analysis of the sexes, it is conceivable than the differences at the extremes are more important that the differences in averages. In mathematics, it is among the most gifted individuals that the sex factor appears most overwhelmingly: seven to eight times more boys than girls score over 600 on the SAT.

The boys also occupy the opposite end of the curve. More males suffer from reading difficulties and scholastic failure. Noted by the sexologist Havelock Ellis, contested by some investigators and supported by others, this twofold male extremism (at both the high and low ends of the curve) underlies Arianna Stassinopoulos's antifeminist analysis. As she writes in *The Female Woman:*

> Men are less average than women. They are the geniuses and the idiots, the giants and the dwarfs. . . . The greater variability of men cannot possibly be explained on environmental grounds, as a simple difference in averages might be. If women are not found in the top positions in society in the same proportions as men because, as Women's Lib claims, they are treated as mentally inferior to men and become so, why are there so many more male idiots? Why are the remedial classes in schools full of boys? Why are the inmates of hospitals for the mentally subnormal predominantly male?. . . The reason why Women's Lib does not mention this conspicuous difference between the sexes is that it can only be explained on purely biological grounds. (349, pp. 28–29)

Is Genius a Male Trait?

This male extremism leads one to pose the question of genius.

Though an irritating issue, that of the sex of genius can scarcely be avoided in a work that attempts to take stock of sex differences. In this regard, the statistics are eloquent. Those of the sexologist Havelock Ellis, to begin with: in a list of 1,030 geniuses, he counted only 55 women (106). The psychologist J.M. Cattell found 32 in a list of 1,000 personalities (64). More recent and more ideologically neutral, the roster of American scientists includes only 7.4 percent women (22 percent in psychology, but only 2.1 percent in physics: the female inferiority in the area of science and technology continues to manifest itself).

More selective but equally eloquent are the figures on the representation of women in scientific academies, though these also reflect an obvious sexism in some cases. Consider that Marie Curie, the symbol of female genius, was never admitted to the Paris Academy of Sciences (while still, it is true, being fully recognized since she received two Nobel Prizes). The first Frenchwoman to be admitted was Yvonne Choquet-Bruhat, in 1980.

In the larger academies this inequality is just as pronounced. In 1982, there were 33 women out of 1,329 members in the American Academy of Science; 29 out of 909 in the British Royal Society; 13 out of 1,100 in the Academy of the Federal Republic of Germany; 21 out of 1,000 in the Deutsche Akademie der Naturforscher Leopoldina in the German Democratic Republic; 3 (and 11 corresponding members) out of 700 members in the Soviet Academy of Sciences; and 3 out of 130 in the French Académie des Sciences—in other words, a figure that in almost all cases fluctuates around 3 percent. In addition, this percentage coincides with another: of the 1,000 researchers most frequently cited by their colleagues in scientific journals, only 27 are women (129). This fateful figure of 3 percent is vastly smaller than the female population pursuing scientific careers (23 percent in the United States in 1980).

All these data produce results comparable to the classic lists of individuals of genius. Annoying, considered in their dry generality, these lists are perhaps even more troublesome when examined in detail. Thus, the 32 women on Cattell's list include 11 queens (whose power was thus due to the system as much as to themselves) and 8 women famous for their beauty or misfortune. And indeed, if one thinks of the names of famous women, it is noteworthy that many of them were wives, intriguers, or exceptional beauties—that is, women more remarkable in terms of their femininity than in terms of their genius. In this area, the figures correspond to popular opinion. P. de Visscher asked 500 people if it were possible for a woman to become "as great a scientific genius as Pasteur or Einstein." Less than 10 percent replied in the affirmative. Yet those surveyed were educated individuals, often with university degrees, many of whom had a background in psychology. Those replying in the affirmative appeared rather embarrassed for evidence and the only names mentioned were those of Marie Curie, Irène Joliot-Curie, and Teresa of Avila, whose identity as a "scientific genius," moreover, is debatable (90).

The question of genius is considerably larger than that of scientific aptitude. For both in the plastic arts and in music, women appear to be singularly excluded from the higher levels of creativity. They are more active in literature. Yet, although there are dozens of well-known female authors, there is not one who can stand among the greatest. To my knowledge, no woman has ever been thought to be as gifted in literature as Shakespeare, Molière or Goethe.

The same is true in painting, where the names that can be cited, non-negligible though they are, cannot be placed on a plane with Leonardo da Vinci, Michelangelo or Goya.

The situation in the area of music is undoubtedly the most irritating of all. There is no female composer comparable to Wagner, Beethoven, Mozart, Bach or Liszt. Girls practice music more than boys; they are especially encouraged in it by their parents, and exhibit, when learning, at least as much aptitude in this area as boys. However, if some become highly skilled performers, none has established herself as a composer of genius. One can try to explain this fact in as many ways as one likes by imagining a diffuse social pressure (even though this pressure would appear to push girls into music), but the results are there—irritatingly so, because it is impossible not to think that a simplistic demagogy would require that they be ignored. Since musical ability appears to be linked to spatial aptitudes, the sex difference in this area could have the same origin as that in mathematics.

The truth is that we cannot at present give a fully satisfactory explanation for these facts, except in the case of aptitude for mathematics and possibly for science. Perhaps there is some general creativity factor with which boys are better equipped. But *it could be something fundamentally different from intelligence.* In effect, males seek to dominate, to shine, to be the first. This need to attain the most admired position carries a masculine connotation, one that, like science itself, seeks to seize things, to master them. It is also one that brings us back to our condition as primates. That is why *this peculiarly male phenomenon, the aptitude for genius, could be merely a way of understanding reality or, more simply, of living, that is less necessary to the female element, more fond of harmony than conquest. But if this is indeed the case, if we must give up the notion that one sex is more talented than the other, it is at the price of recognizing the male taste for domination.* In other words, as will have been guessed, it amounts to discarding one unpleasant conclusion only to adopt another.

Different Strategies to Apprehend Reality

Is this to say that women are less intelligent than men? That is precisely the sort of assertion one must avoid making. Most studies of intelligence quotients have found no significant sex differences. On the other hand, what appears to be increasingly certain is that the sexes adopt different intellectual strategies to apprehend and master reality.

This is even true in the animal world, as can be observed among the chimpanzees of Tai National Park in the Ivory Coast. These animals use clubs and stones to open various kinds of nuts. This is one of several known cases of rudimentary tool use in the animal world. Researchers are no longer very surprised to find such cultural manifestations among primates. On the other hand, two Swiss ethologists, Christophe and Hedwinge Boesch of the University of Zurich, have made an astonishing discovery: the males and females do not use the hammer and anvil in the same way (49). The females are almost the only ones who open the very hard panda nuts. They are also the only ones who crack kola nuts directly in the trees. This performance implies premeditation, for while a conveniently located branch is used as an anvil in this case, the hammer must be selected *before* climbing into the tree. This suggests that female primates may be more cultivated than males and, by the same token, that in the lineage of our ancestors, they too could have participated in the development of tools—a hypothesis that prehistorians generally tend to underrate. But beyond the validation of the female, this discovery carries us still further, for it suggests that the two sexes may use different strategies to master the world in which they live.

The same situation prevails in man and woman. The two partners use their cerebral mechanisms differently in order to solve problems; yet both succeed in correctly mastering their environment. But they do so by following different routes, which for woman, it is correct to say, involve a greater intervention of emotive factors and for man a greater reliance on abstraction.

The studies of cerebral asymmetry help us to better understand the nature of the differences in intellectual strategy between the sexes. Thus, in Sandra Witelson's view, "It is perhaps more difficult for women than men to perform two cognitive tasks at the same time. It may be more difficult for women than men to deal with spatial aspects of the environment, for example to decide which road to take while talking at the same time." This is due to more complete hemispheric connection. For men, on the other hand, since the two hemispheres form more independent neurological systems, it is easier to perform two separate tasks at once. Sandra Witelson says, "I cannot cite any studies that deal with this problem or that supply useful data regarding it. Nevertheless, my personal experience along with anecdotes concerning other people lead me to think it is possible that women have more difficulty performing certain tasks simultaneously."

But here too it is important not to rush into necessarily interpreting matters in terms of superiority and inferiority. "Such a difference," writes Witelson, "if it is real, could also be an advantage to women in the sense that they would be better able to focus their attention on one specific task at a time, which can be an advantage" (397, p. 296).

Another highly eminent specialist, Jerre Levy, stresses the greater linkage in women between the processes of perception and those of verbal communication. "In this view," she explains, "females would show deficiencies, relative to males, in reading maps because of their sensitivity to the radical differences between the world of experience and its representation as abstract lines on a map; for males the invariants between maps and the world they represent would be easily perceived since the world in the first place was encoded as a set of abstract relationships." This relative weakness is compensated for by an advantage, since "the superiority of females to males in understanding the social world would derive from their ability to note, remember, and integrate a wealth of information that is relevant for appreciating social interactions" (206).

Man would thus appear, on average, to be more gifted at perceiving the physical world and woman that of social relations.

From this a number of applied conclusions can be deduced—for example, notes Jerre Levy, with regard to communication between the sexes. It is common for men to ask their partners, "What are you getting at? Get to the point." Or, not infrequently, they find female judgments to be lacking in rational justification. And when these turn out to be correct, the male attributes this to luck or female intuition. Such incomprehension undoubtedly explains the terrible misogynous statement of Erasmus: "Woman is an inept and ridiculous animal. . . . Woman is always woman, that is, stupid."

The truth could well be entirely different. If the male cerebral machine is structured to reason by way of abstractions, it may be that it has difficulty perceiving certain important elements. One could just as well say that it is by nature, by congenital inadequacy, incapable of achieving the performances of the other sex. Inversely, capable of directly understanding situations that require complex thinking for men, women would reveal themselves to be inept at formulating the whole in abstract terms (which moreover are generally useless, at least in social life). This example has the advantage not only of bringing us back to a concrete situation, but also and perhaps above all of making clear that it is indeed a question of different intellectual strategies, which are equally effective overall (that is, more functional in certain cases and less so in others), and which consequently do not lend themselves to value judgments in terms of superiority and inferiority.

One may a priori be shocked to learn that there are different ways of apprehending the world. But knowledge itself is a process of selection, in which the mind emphasizes the things that it judges to be relevant (73). There is no knowledge without the elimination of useless data, which form a sort of intellectual background noise from which it is necessary to select.

From this standpoint, one can well imagine that men and women tend not to judge exactly the same elements to be relevant, that they eliminate at least some different data in order to see clearly, while both achieving a real understanding. Just as it is possible to go from one point in a forest to another by following different paths.

9

The Circle of Life

If the human brain is gendered, if the differences that we believe are so superficial are so deeply rooted in our anatomy, does this mean that everything is fixed for all eternity? This is undoubtedly what feminists fear most of all.

In fact, things are not that simple. *Biological does not mean immutable*. One can manipulate and modify life. Moreover, a number of researchers have already done just that with animals.

Modifying the Sex of the Brain

The first findings in this area date back to early in the century. In 1916, the Canadian researcher Frank Lillie noticed that genetically female calves sometimes resemble and behave like males. The common feature of such calves is the presence of a male twin. They are called "freemartin" animals. Their condition results from the male hormone secreted by their brothers, which masculinizes them in the womb.

Since this discovery, freemartin guinea pigs, rats, dogs, and monkeys have been brought into the world by injecting testosterone, the male hormone, into pregnant females. In 1959, this approach enabled two researchers at the University of Kansas, William Young and Robert Goy, to grasp the essential. Female guinea pigs dosed with testosterone during fetal life displayed not only a male appearance but male behavior as well, mounting other females and dominating groups. It was then, says Goy, that "we realized that we had changed the sex of the guinea pig's brain" (377). Just as the injection of male hormone masculinizes a female brain, the grafting of male nerve cells can masculinize a female's behavior (10).

81

A Reciprocal Influence

At this point, all the data fit together like a well-constructed puzzle, from Julianne Imperato-McGinley's evidence on sex changes in Santo Domingo to the findings of neurophysiology. The sex hormones affect not only the anatomical development of the reproductive organs but also that of certain brain structures, such as the hypothalamus and the amygdala. Evidence of this influence has even been found at the microcosmic level, that of the cell membranes, where Bruce McEwen and other researchers have identified receptors for the sex hormones. This indicates that the brain possesses natural anchoring points for the sex hormones—that it is made to interact with them.

This interaction takes place at two principal times in life: during a first hormonal discharge in the womb, which causes the brain and genitals to develop in a certain direction, and during a second discharge at puberty.

Such is the essential schema. Many hypotheses have been advanced to explain its details. Perhaps the most brilliant is that of the late N. Geschwind, a leading specialist in this area. Geschwind noticed a curious association between two apparently unrelated phenomena: left-handed people are more likely to suffer from auto-immune diseases (which occur when the immune system turns against the organism instead of defending it). According to Geschwind, testosterone contributes to the differentiation of the two sides of the brain. As we have already seen, the two sides of the brain fulfill different functions, and women's brains are less asymmetrical than men's.

According to Geschwind, testosterone is ordinarily responsible for the development of cerebral asymmetry in men; but if secreted in excessive quantity, it inhibits this process. This, he proposes, is exactly what happens in left-handed people. In support of his thesis, Geschwind points out that most left-handed people are male. This would accord with a hypothesis implicating the male hormone. Testosterone, Geschwind believes, is also responsible for producing auto-immune diseases by its effect on certain types of white blood cells. This would link the phenomenon of left-handedness, various auto-immune diseases, and also certain sex differences: *impregnated with testosterone, the male brain is more asymmetrical.* (If Geschwind's hypothesis is correct, among left-handers the hormonal excess should also cause an anomaly leading to a dominance of

the right side of the brain in certain activities involving language.)
(131, 224)

Male Hormones and Mathematical Aptitude

Can we connect these findings and hypotheses to psychology
and—why not—explain the male superiority in mathematics?

A study published in the *New England Journal of Medicine* is
encouraging in this regard. In this study, Daniel Hier and his colleagues report their observations of adolescent boys stricken with idio-
pathic hypogonadism, a condition that manifests itself by a low level of
androgens (the male hormones). Boys with this condition scored considerably lower on intelligence tests than individuals with normal
androgen levels (154). At this point, the data fit together reasonably
well: the male hormones, which endocrinologists have shown interact
with the brain, may confer greater spatial aptitudes with regard to mathematical ability.

Camilla Benbow and Julian Stanley, the Johns Hopkins University
psychologists who have studied the male superiority in mathematics,
became interested in Geschwind's hypothesis. To test it, they adminis-
tered a questionnaire to the most gifted students, those with scores over
700 on the SAT (52, 190). They discovered that 20 percent of these
gifted students were left-handed, more than twice the proportion of left-
handers in the general population. Even more striking, 60 percent of
the students suffered from various auto-immune ailments (principally
allergies), more than five times the figure for the general population.
(Another characteristic of these mathematically gifted individuals: 70
percent were nearsighted.) These results accord well with Geschwind's
hypothesis on the connection between testosterone, auto-immune diseases, and left-handedness.

Is Intelligence a By-product of Sex?

It may seem strange, even shocking, to realize that the brain is
influenced by sex as much as it influences sexuality. After all, affairs
of the mind are ordinarily placed on the highest plane. We would like
all other things to be subject to them. Furthermore, we would like to
locate everything important in the most evolved part of the brain—the
brain of the highly perfected primates we are, which is responsible for

our intellectual life. Alas, the work of Paul MacLean (popularized by Arthur Koestler) shows that this is not the case. In reality, we have three brains in one, and the most primal brain, inherited from our reptilian past, rules our emotional life without obeying the most intelligent one.

Reflection on sexual behavior in a sense justifies this shocking fact. It is definitely normal for sexuality to be stronger sometimes than rationality, explaining the countless follies great and small committed in the name of Love. What, after all, is sexuality—and sociobiology rightly insists on this point—if not a means to ensure reproduction, the transmittal of the genes? It is, in other words, the most essential fact of all, since without it we would not even exist. Sexuality is therefore vital; it is more necessary than intelligence. In a sense, intelligence is just one of the many strategies established by evolution to encourage the continuity of the genes that have proved to be most effective. From this standpoint, intelligence is a by-product, although a prestigious one, of sexuality. Are there grounds for astonishment, then, if intelligence is so largely subordinate to sexuality?

The Circle of Life

Thus, the data of very different sciences are united in a coherent fashion: sexology, endocrinology, neurophysiology, psychology, genetics, evolutionary theory, and sociobiology.

It all begins with one small difference—a difference at the level of the sex chromosomes. That is to say a difference, in man, involving a single one of 46 chromosomes, and which, primarily through the influence of hormonal secretions, modifies various aspects of the developing fetus, and the brain in particular. The brain in turn influences sexual and other behaviors and encourages reproduction, that is, the transmittal of the genes and the consequent perpetuation of chromosomal sex differences. We have thus come full circle. From the genes to the brain and back again, passing by way of hormones and sexuality, all the elements of life are united in a single schema.

The Role of Culture

But what about society? What about culture? Does this schema reduce them to a peripheral role? Assuredly not. But one must assign them to their proper sphere. They are part of a system outside of which they would serve no purpose; for, it can never be repeated too often, a culture is first and foremost something that confers significance on human activities. This indicates that society and culture are in part "secreted" by the mental or affective life of human beings, and, above all, that they influence people by amplifying certain elements of the system that constitutes their life cycle.

For example, it is true that if boys behave like boys and girls like girls, this is, in the first instance, because of hormonal secretions that set the tone. But it is also true that girls and boys are seen as such by their parents and peers, which can undoubtedly accentuate the phenomenon. Thus, girls are dressed in skirts and boys in pants. But—and this is the essential point—*the cultural process operates here in support of a biological difference.* It does not create the difference itself. The cultural process accentuates the biological difference because, in the final analysis, it is biologically advantageous to do so—meaning that the behaviors underlying it confer a greater chance of reproductive success.

The same situation prevails in the case of language. Not only does language often carry a latent sexism denounced by feminists (278), but verbal communication (and nonverbal communication as well) bears witness to the dissymmetry of the sexes. Thus, men tend to interrupt the persons they are speaking with more often. No doubt they thereby attempt to display their dominance. Moreover, women manifest more pauses in conversation and ask more questions (277). These differences in behavior relative to language begin in childhood. One can, to be sure, regard them as instruments of domination—and in a sense they are—but at bottom, cultural practices merely accentuate an existing predisposition; they are not its cause.

The essential adjustment we must make in our thinking in this area is now in sight. *There is no essential difference between the cultural and the biological.* Each proceeds from the other. Moreover, the cultural is not the opposite of the biological, as is generally presumed (73). The cultural characteristically works in the same direction as the biological. It too was set in place to encourage the essential—namely, reproductive success. Like intelligence, culture is a by-product of this imperative. The purpose of culture is not to replace the circle of life but to make it rotate more efficiently. That is why, far from eliminating the effects of biological differences, it accentuates them.

10

Proof by Pathology

Just as genetics developed through the study of mutations and physiology through that of pathology, research on sex differences is indebted to the study of deviancy. Abnormalities make it easier to grasp the normal, which is, so to speak, transparent to scientific investigation. Frequently, a detour is necessary in order to render it visible. In this sense the pathological is not the annihilation of the healthy but its unmasking. It represents the exaggeration of one element at the expense of others or (which amounts to the same thing) the inhibition or cancellation of a particular element. We have already seen this in regard to homosexuality, which in some respects exacerbates masculinity and femininity more than it cancels them. With this perspective in mind, we can profitably approach the data on the contrasting psychiatry of the sexes.

Male Fragility

An initial fact in this area is that male fragility is visible from infancy on. *Females, physically the stronger sex, are also the mentally resistant sex* (104, 140). Among children under 14 in the U.S., more than two and a half times as many boys as girls are admitted to hospitals on psychiatric grounds. In the 14- to 17-year-old age bracket, the number of admissions is approximately equal between the sexes; thereafter, it is slightly reversed (1.4 girls to each boy).

This overrepresentation of males among the psychologically disturbed also prevails in the American black community and in European nations. Young males appear to be particularly fragile with regard to behavioral difficulties, enuresis, encopresis, and learning disabilities. Inversely, anorexia is ten times more common in girls than in boys.

The cause of this male weakness in childhood is not known with certainty. If this weakness is considered in conjunction with susceptibility to ailments other than mental ones, it is tempting to view it as an aspect of a possible male fragility caused by the presence of a single X chromosome. It is conceivable (as we have seen in the case of spatial aptitudes, but this time in a negative sense) that this phenomenon is caused by deleterious recessive genes (that is, genes that do not express themselves when associated with another gene that dominates them). Unable to profit from a gene, located on a second X chromosome, capable of exercising a compensating effect, males victimized by a "bad" gene would necessarily be more susceptible to disease. In contrast, females could "ransom" themselves with their second X chromosome.

Hypotheses based on social factors should also not be overlooked. Presumably, if the male sex is the more favored one on account of sexism, females should display a corresponding psychological weakness. But it is also possible that, because of greater pressures to succeed, fear of failure may create even more difficulties among males.

Be that as it may, male weakness remains very evident with respect to mental retardation: twice as many men as women are mentally retarded.

Crime is a Male Specialty

Another male deviation involves aggression. Violent crime, a pathological form of this normally beneficial behavior, is largely a male affair (395). The chromosome of crime is the Y chromosome present in a double dose (the individual thus being XYY). Despite efforts to downplay this phenomenon, it remains clearly evident. All XYY males are not criminals and all criminals are not XYY's (indeed, only a small minority of criminals are), but it is equally clear that an XYY individual is more likely to commit crimes of impulsive violence than a normal XY male or a victim of Klinefelter's syndrome, an XXY individual, who is predisposed to various forms of deviance but not to violent ones.

That violent crime is a male specialty is obvious. As a classic work of criminology points out, "Sex status is of greater statistical significance in differentiating criminals from noncriminals than any other trait" (353, p. 126). Moreover, female crime often appears to be a result of a masculinization of woman's behavior.

There are social reasons for this lesser female criminality as well, starting with the fact that women may have fewer opportunities for killing, as a result of their more confined sphere of activity. In addition, being held in a state of greater dependency, it may be more difficult for women to externalize violent tendencies. No doubt such arguments should be taken into account. But one must also note that male criminality is not merely a transition from impulse to action: it corresponds to a psychological predisposition that tests indicate is more pronounced in man than in woman, which involves a greater taste for aggression and a far less pronounced tendency toward pacifism. All of this tends to suggest that criminality is a pathological exaggeration of masculinity.

PMS and Female Violence

Another indicator pointing in this direction is the existence of a female violence that is appreciably different in nature (376), reflecting woman's greater dependence on her body. This female violence appears to be a pathology of internalization of the world, whereas male violence appears to be a pathology of its externalization (cf. 111).

On this subject, the case of premenstrual syndrome or PMS is suggestive. A lot of ink has been spilled over this affliction in the last few years.* The condition was described by Franck as early as 1931. Premenstrual syndrome is a state of tension that precedes menstruation. It must be presumed that the tension in question appears to be normal or at least "in the nature of things," since most of the attention it has received has been relatively recent. Nevertheless, contemporary data on PMS appear to be fairly disturbing. According to the International Health Foundation, 77 percent of women suffer from some degree of PMS. Cerutti's study places this figure at 82 percent, of whom 43 percent suffer from PMS slightly, 24 percent moderately, and 15 percent severely. The chief symptom of PMS is heightened irritability. Other symptoms include pressure in the breasts, depression, weight gain, headaches, pelvic pain, etc.

This phenomenon, which underscores the relationship between hormonal state and mood, presents female variability in a new light.

*Cf. 151, 194, 261.

Research by R.H. Moos enables one to acquire a fairly precise idea of what is involved. Dr. Alain Tamborini, who recently opened a specialized practice on PMS at the Boucicaut hospital in Paris, summarizes Moos's findings as follows:

> Sense of "well-being" and activity are maximal during ovulation; anxiety and aggressivity are minimal at this time and increase over the course of the premenstrual period. The physical symptoms follow the same curve as the psychological ones, anxiety and aggression. Moos has thus established a certain parallelism between physical and psychological symptoms.

"Even unconscious moods," Tamborini reports, "appear to be cyclical, as indicated by several studies on the subjects of dreams" (358).

If PMS has become so fashionable of late it is also, and perhaps primarily, because it has been cited in several highly publicized legal cases. In Britain, PMS has been treated as a mitigating circumstance in crimes committed by women. Thanks in particular to the testimony of Katharina Dalton of the PMS clinic in London, known as "the guru of premenstrual syndrome," a number of courts have held that the perpetrators of violent crimes acted under the influence of uncontrollable pressures. They were no longer themselves. Katharina Dalton goes so far as to speak of "temporary insanity." She thereby resuscitates the old notions of the Italian Cesare Lombroso on female criminality, which according to him can be explained by biological factors that generate changes in mood (209).

Women are More Susceptible to Depression

Premenstrual syndrome underscores the relationship of the psyche to the female body. At the same time, it illustrates the importance of emotivity for woman.

That woman is more the prisoner of her emotional life than man is also suggested by statistics on depression. Moreover, depression is not without links to premenstrual syndrome, as has recently been shown (44).

In this domain it was once again a woman, Maggie Scarf, who shook up the conventional wisdom, by devoting a lengthy work, *Unfinished Business*, to this vast problem (321). Maggie Scarf's point of departure is the fact that women suffer 2 to 6 times more depressions than men. This is, if anything, a rather banal observation: it suffices to look around oneself to witness the ravages of female depression (284, 378, 379). This female tendency to depression is found in all age brackets. As Dr. T. Lempérière and his colleagues at the Louis Mourier hospital in Colombes state, "Depression appears to be a preferred mode of expression of conflicts in woman; man tends to express his difficulties by adopting pathological behaviors that carry a more masculine social connotation, such as alcoholism and antisocial behaviors" (198).

Female susceptibility to depression is thus an established fact. But it has usually been explained in terms of preconceived notions that focus exclusively on the circumstances of women's lives. Professional careers and lifestyles similar to men's should therefore take care of the problem. Alas, Maggie Scarf has examined her data: there are as many depressions among working women as among women in general. Could this fact, then, be a consequence of menopause among women approaching fifty? Not in the least: the most frequently afflicted are women around the age of thirty.

The figures obstinately suggest a different cause, one that is both psychological and biological. By their very nature, women may have a greater need for attachment to others. As a result, they would be more vulnerable in the event of a rupture in their personal relations, such as the end of an affair, divorce, the death of a loved one, or the departure of their children from home—events that are frequently associated with the onset of depression. All these considerations accord well with Sandra Witelson's hypothesis that, by the very fact of their brain structure, women are less able than men to dissociate their emotional and rational behaviors.

To such considerations, Maggie Scarf adds a variety of observations borrowed directly from ethology (the study of animal and human behavior). Numerous studies indicate that women are by nature more prone than men to attachment to those around them. This tendency appears as of birth: for example, female babies react more quickly than male babies to photographs of human faces. From these findings to the conclusion that such a capacity is innate, that it is inscribed in our genes, is just a short step, which Maggie Scarf takes and genetics appears to confirm (25).

Recently, such theories on female depression have been reinforced by a number of biochemical studies. Bruce McEwen and his colleagues have found sex differences in rats' brains in the levels of serotonin, a chemical that plays an important role in communications between nerve cells (119) and is implicated in depression.

At this point, all the evidence fits together: everyday observation, psychological data, brain anatomy, endocrinology, biochemistry, etc.

Is there a male equivalent to depression? Alcoholism, which is more common among men than among women, may play such a role. This behavior would thus constitute a sort of antidepressive therapy. A study among the Amish, who reject the use of alcohol, has found that, in the absence of alcoholism, depression occurs equally often in men and women. It is also worth noting that addictions in general are 4 to 5 times more common among males.

The Confrontation of Normalities

The contrasting psychiatry of the sexes is of more than anecdotal interest, for it highlights the nature of the two sexes. It also constitutes the ultimate illustration of the logical problems that masculinity and femininity can pose for the adepts of feminism.

Consider the standard psychiatric classifications. The bible in this area is the third edition of the *Diagnostic and Statistical Manual of Mental Disorders* put out by the American Psychiatric Association, usually referred to as "DSM-III." In one sense, DSM-III is a masterpiece of sexism: it takes gender into consideration, in that its definitions of psychological normality differ for men and women. As a logical consequence of this, there is also a disjuncture in its definitions of psychological abnormality.

A consistent antisexism would require the adoption of unisexist criteria. But this would produce a manifestly artificial increase in the number of pathological cases.

Paradoxically, some feminists have criticized DSM-III on the opposite ground: that it does not take sex differences into account *enough*. Such is the rationale for a crusade recently waged by Marcie Kaplan, a Rutgers University psychologist (152, 179). Kaplan, objecting to statistics that indicate there are more cases of insanity among women than among men (in adults), accuses DSM-III of gender bias. She maintains that DSM-III aims in a sense at the suppression of femininity. Pure masculinity, she says, "is not clinically suspect," whereas pronounced femininity is (179).

Thus, Dependent Personality Disorder, which is typically female, is defined as pathological. (Always woman is considered "submissive and imitative," but this time these traits are seen through feminist eyes.) In contrast, the term "Independent Personality Disorder" is not applied to the behavior of the male employee who thinks of nothing but work and career and without a trace of emotion asks others to follow him passively. Similar considerations, says Kaplan, apply to hysteria, which she views as a form of excited dramatization, a female specialty.

As excessive as they undoubtedly are, Marcie Kaplan's ideas highlight a basic problem: ·how to define the limits of social normality when, because of the fact of gender, there are at least two different types of normality. But the solution viewed from the perspective of egalitarian feminism is fraught with inescapable contradictions. For example, shall we deny the existence of hysteria in women, or shall we affirm that hysterical women are normal? Unless one acknowledges the naturalness of sex differences, one is trapped in the same vicious circle as Marcie Kaplan. Seeking to deny the existence of a merely *relative* difference in the number of hospitalized individuals, she ends up radicalizing the difference to the point of making it an *absolute* one. Antisexism thus becomes hypersexism, furnishing the attentive observer with a veritable proof by the absurd. The pathological, we have said, makes it possible to understand the normal. Often, and quite involuntarily, antisexism makes it possible to highlight the reality of sex differences.

11

Male and Female Modalities

In the course of our analysis, we have deepened our understanding of the question of sex differences by restating it in different terms. Our search led us first of all to reject the feminism-sexism dichotomy, as the most simplistic reductionism formulates it via the question of sexual inequality. The reply to such a question is clearly of little importance. It is more a matter of temperament than of science. The real question lies elsewhere. For as Count Keyserling said, "it is just as fundamentally ridiculous to speak of the superiority of man or woman as to speak of the superiority of the positive or negative electric pole" (185).

Clearly, between men and women there are points in common and elements of difference. Just as clearly, many men display relatively feminine traits and many women relatively masculine ones. In consequence, one should attempt neither, by a dangerous stylistic exercise, to deny the reality of the differences, nor to make them into absolutes, but simply to take note of their statistical existence and, above all—for a catalogue of differences in this area presents little more than anecdotal interest—to explain their significance.

The Strategy of Penetration

What emerges from this inquiry is that there is a way of conducting oneself in relation to others and the world that is more male and a way that is more female. This is not at all to say—my thought is essentially opposed to this kind of typologism—that men systematically act in one way and women in another. In effect, the only reality is the tremendous variety of individual behavior. But the extent of the possibilities does not rule out the identification of tendencies, just as one can identify political tendencies in spite of the diversity of individual opinions.

What lies behind the concepts of masculinity and femininity is not a collection of unrelated traits to be catalogued like objects in an exhibition, but groups of predispositions that make it possible to define two different types of relationship to the environment. These represent two strategies for apprehending the world that are equally effective on balance, rather than a single voyage that can be completed more quickly by one route than another. Behind male "superiority" in sports, professional life, and possibly science, what appears is less a real advantage than a male tendency to desire to be the first, to behave like a creature obsessed with competition. Psychologically, the male spends his life in an arena. "Competition is the sphere of the male sex," writes the feminist anthropologist Evelyn Reed on this subject (287). Man thus appears as the adept of a sort of aggressive exhibitionism that is manifestly inherited from the parade behaviors of his mammalian ancestors. In all things, it is the male who exhibits himself.

This is even true for species in which the female is dominant. Consider the lemurs of Madagascar. Among these animals, the female dominates, in the sense that, for instance, she eats first. But it is the male who parades upon meeting his conspeciates. Sometimes the exasperated female strikes him to send him to go play somewhere else, but he cannot stop himself from seeking attention. In the course of a human life, one could not even begin to describe all the parades dear to the heart of the Homo sapiens male, a veritable no-holds-barred exhibitionist: at the office, on the beach, in the home, and above all on the highway. But, just as among lemurs, the whole point of the exercise is to display oneself. The hierarchy visible on the outside is often reversed in domestic life. As Sarah Hrdy writes, "The publicly acclaimed emperor may be ruled by his wife at home; a sated tyrant may lose a wedge of meat when matched against a particularly hungry minion; and the richest or most powerful male may not beget the most children if his wives are routinely unfaithful" (157, p. 3). Even in those activities that are regarded as most serious or most intellectual, the need for parading and competition expresses and exacerbates itself. How, for example, is one to interpret scientific competition for the Nobel Prize if not as an intellectual manifestation of this imperative? This competition, moreover, is a beneficial one. The crusty old professor, the with-it young researcher, the Nobel-obsessed pioneer, are all so many examples which indicate that intelligence is not necessarily an end in itself but rather a means to be the strongest; to be a male primate parading to the point of exhibitionism: a being unable to comprehend the world except by trying to conquer, possess, and penetrate it.

Science: A Male Enterprise?

The British historian Brian Easlea, writing from an intendedly feminist viewpoint, has devoted an entire work to *Science and Sexual Oppression* (96). Easlea's central thesis is that *science is in essence male; it excludes the female dimension and leads to its domination by masculine values.*

At first glance, this idea may appear gratuitously provocative. But how does it fit the facts? Clearly, science has largely been a male affair.* We have already implied as much in raising the question of genius. To be sure, one can cite the names of several major female scientists: Marie Curie and Irène Joliot-Curie among physicists (let us note in regard to these two symbols of female genius that both were married to eminent scientists), Barbara McClintock, who opened a new path for genetic science, and Rosalind Yallow, who did the same for physiology. But all the greatest names belong to the male sex—Copernicus, Galileo, Newton, Pasteur, Darwin, Einstein, etc. Clearly, in an enlarged list of eminent persons women would still only constitute a minority.** Furthermore, in many cases the female presence would only serve to reinforce the masculine tenor of the whole. Must one cite in this regard Margaret Cavendish, Duchess of Newcastle, the author of several scientific works in the seventeenth century, who affirmed that "One must not expect that I will write with as much discernment or spirit as men; for I am of the female sex, and nature has formed the minds of that sex with very cold and soft elements." Thus, renowned female scholars may have been the first to recognize their own "inferiority." No doubt, as such declarations lead one to believe,

*Cf. 4, 58, 60, 77, 78, 116-118, 144, 161, 181-183, 188, 215, 219, 222, 237, 257, 267, 271, 276, 291, 302-304, 309, 326, 342, 354, 373, 384.

**There can be no question of establishing a ranking of the greatest scholars, but it is better to avoid the temptation of certain feminists, who risk themselves in comparisons that can only serve as anti-demonstrations. Thus one reads in a recent work about women in scholarship: "One speaks of Pythagoras but not of his female followers, of Newton but not of Emilie du Châtelet, of Watson and Crick but not of Rosalind Franklin" (80, p. 84). To associate the name of Newton with that of Voltaire's mistress, although she was a highly cultivated woman who wrote a fine essay about the father of gravitation, is in reality to highlight, not the equivalence of the sexes, but their disparity.

there is something very stereotyped in these notions, which merely reflects a then-dominant way of thinking. But how can one fail to see, on a more penetrating level of analysis (if one may so speak), that the scientific approach seeks to conquer and dominate the universe; that it is an active process, in the image of the male who naturally occupies the most dynamic and externally oriented role, the woman being more oriented towards her personal universe; that science is effectuating, that it sets forces in motion? Think of the conquest of fire, of nuclear power (97), even of life itself through modern biotechnologies. This mode of investing in the world, of penetrating the universe, has been celebrated by many of the great philosophers of science, starting with Descartes, who wished to make men "the masters and possessors of nature." Hence Karl Stern's judgment that Cartesianism represents "a pure masculinization of thought."

Science thus confounds itself with a masculine mode of thought, a means for man to penetrate the universe as he penetrates woman through sex. Sartre said exactly this in *Being and Nothingness:* "To see is to *deflower.* . . . Knowledge is at once a *penetration* and a *surface caress*" (319, p. 638). Conversely, feminine values, based on affectivity and, why not, on collusion with the world, find themselves excluded from this manner of seeing. Under the circumstances, are there grounds for astonishment if scientific research leads to the atom bomb rather than to universal peace!

These reflections inevitably call to mind certain schemas that are popular among contemporary critics of scientific development. This is a somewhat paradoxical movement, in that it affects research milieus far more than the public at large, which retains immense confidence in science and scientists. Its target is of course capitalism, engine of destruction in the name of a ruthless and greedy quest for power, but also "scientific" socialism. Brian Easlea very judiciously observes that in this regard Marx and his followers display none of the sentimental utopianism of Fourier and Saint-Simon, but rather a sense of masculine scienticity. In the words of a Herbert Marcuse, "science, through its method and concepts, has produced a world in which the domination of nature is bound up with the domination of man," and furthermore, "woman literally incarnates the promise of peace, joy, and an end to violence." That is why feminism cohabits harmoniously with the hostility to scientific development that is particularly prominent among the self-declared "radical scientists." In the view of this school, science, like language (278), is an instrument of male domination.*

Perhaps all this lends too much importance to an intellectual fashion that is obviously excessive. Yet how can we fail to see that *its excess is not wholly imaginary, but a caricature*. It reflects an underlying reality that, though certainly more nuanced, is authentic. Paradoxically, this feminist approach, based on egalitarianism, leads to a recognition of the reality of the differences between man and woman. Moreover, it supports the stereotype that has been rediscovered by contemporary neuroanatomists: woman has more difficulty separating intellect and emotion. Thus, what was intended to be a feminist mode of thought ends by converging with an approach that is a priori more suspected of sexism and which gives pride of place to the difference. Finally, what is confirmed here once more is that men and women do not use their cognitive capacities in the same way: they do not utilize the same method of confronting reality.

Moreover, women have made major contributions to knowledge in research areas that call for relatively little of an extreme spirit of dissection or conceptualization but rather a taste for direct observation. I am thinking in particular of a discipline relative to many of the subjects treated in this book, the study of primates in their natural settings. Jane Goodall, the most famous representative of the world of primatology, who pioneered the study of chimpanzees in the wild, is only the best-known name in this field. One can also cite Dian Fossey, who lived with the mountain gorillas; Sarah Hrdy, with her studies of the langurs of India; Jane Lancaster, etc. In my view, it is significant that this type of research places a premium on sharp powers of observation and, above all, that it involves an absence of intervention in nature. The researcher is effective in proportion as he or she traumatizes the environment less and does not seek to dissect or mutilate the object of study. Women's interest in botany in the nineteenth century can be explained in similar terms (3, 312), as can the female presence in ethnography (Margaret Mead, Ruth Benedict, Françoise l'Héritier, etc.). In all these cases, the object is to be at one with the world, to apprehend it while respecting its existing harmony. Nothing similar exists in molecular biology, nuclear physics or medicine, or even in mathematics—a discipline that may not involve a spirit of dissection, but which carries the investigator far from the everyday world and

*Cf. 9, 43, 54, 114, 115, 145, 158-160, 167, 220, 236, 313, 346, 367.

plunges him into the heart of abstract conceptualization.

Even a female researcher like Barbara McClintock, discovering a hard-to-observe phenomenon, jumping genes, fifty years ahead of any-one else, does not escape this rule. In effect, this Nobel Prize winner said that she proceeded in her work "by listening to the material," by "feeling it" (181). In this respect, her work on maize differs radically from that of the modern manipulators of heredity, who have rediscovered the same phenomenon through more abstract methods of investigation.

Is this to say that the sexes' ways of thinking are completely different? Assuredly not. Clearly, it is only a question here of habitual modes of behavior that do not apply to all members of the population. Manifestly, some women behave according to the male model and vice versa. It is thus merely a question of statistical truths that should be approached with caution. Let us therefore conclude simply that it is possible to apprehend the world according to different modalities, one of which is more male and the other more female. The harmonious collaboration of these two constitutes human knowledge as a whole. That is why it is no longer a question of comparing or attempting to oversimplify sex differences, but of taking the measure of the complexity of the situation and adopting a nuanced evaluation.

Harmony, "Key to the Feminine Universe"

The British philosopher and economist John Stuart Mill (1806–1873) had already very well perceived the significance of these differences in intellectual strategy and in what ways they could benefit knowledge as a whole. An ardent defender of the female cause who called for women's right to work, vote, receive an education, and equality, Mill wrote in *The Subjection of Women*: "this gravitation of women's minds to the present, to the real, to the actual fact, while in its exclusiveness it is a source of errors, is also a most useful counteractive of the contrary error." Mill denounced the straying of speculative minds incapable of perceiving the "objective fact" and which not only neglect "the contradiction which outward facts oppose to their theories, but lose sight of the legitimate purpose of speculation altogether and let their speculative faculties go astray into regions not peopled with real beings, animate or inanimate, even idealized, but with personified shadows created by the illusions of metaphysics or by the mere entanglement of words." Thus the conclusion of this philosopher, himself deeply in love with a feminist:

> Hardly anything can be of greater value to a man of theory and speculation who employs himself not in collecting materials of knowledge by observation, but in working them up by processes of thought into comprehensive truths of science and laws of conduct, than to carry on his speculations in the companionship, and under the criticism, of a really superior woman. There is nothing comparable to it for keeping his thoughts within the limits of real things, and the actual facts of nature. A woman seldom runs wild after an abstraction.

Hence, an intellectual safety valve but also a human one, because of "her more lively interest in the present feelings of persons, which makes her consider first of all, in anything which claims to be applied to practice, in what manner persons will be affected by it." This leads her to shy away from

> speculation which loses sight of individuals, and deals with things as if they existed for the benefit of some imaginary entity, some mere creation of the mind, not resolvable into the feelings of living beings. Women's thoughts are thus as useful in giving reality to those of thinking men, as men's thoughts in giving width and largeness to those of women. In depth, as distinguished from breadth, I greatly doubt if even now, women, compared with men, are at any disadvantage. (240, pp. 134-135)

From this perspective, the relative female weakness in science appears in a new light, which is no longer that of inferiority, of a vision of woman as a near-equal of man—the too frequent translation of feminist ideology. It is a way, instead, of highlighting two different ways of being in relation to the universe. To the male strategy, based on penetration, the female approach opposes greater collusion with the world, a greater search for harmony. Hence, indeed, a relative rejection of scientific disciplines based on the dissection of reality. But hence, too, a tendency toward political conservatism, a hostility to war, a rejection of violence (72, 94, 113), etc.

No doubt it is significant that today ones sees female and feminist writers themselves insisting on this point. As it is significant to find the same ambivalence in the couple of Sartre and de Beauvoir. What do we see here? On one hand a Sartre driven by his ethic to conquer the natural, always ready to denounce life. On the other a Simone de Beauvoir who, adopting pagan accents, celebrates the "manifold splendor" of life.

The author of *The Second Sex* establishes herself as a precursor by grasping the link between the feminine and the sense of harmony. "The notion of harmony," she writes, "is one of the keys to the feminine universe; it implies perfection in immobility, the immediate justification of every element as part of the whole and its passive participation in the totality." This is so clear as to seem strange. For to recognize that one sex has a particular sense of harmony is also to admit the existence of sex differences—and even to amplify them.

Internal versus External Space

In woman, the search for harmony is also an *internalization,* a tendency to center space on oneself. In this sense, one could say that even little girls have a homebody side. This has been very well demonstrated by the psychoanalyst Erik Erikson. In the course of a study at the University of California, he arranged to have children between the ages of 10 and 12 come by twice a year for tests. The children were given toys representing families, policemen, Indians, animals, and furniture, as well as an assortment of blocks. They were asked to construct a scene taking place in a movie studio and to explain it through a story. Erik Erikson's initial interest was not in sex differences but in children's attitudes toward construction. Nevertheless, a major sex difference soon became apparent: in Erikson's words, "the girls emphasize inner space, the boys outer space" (111, p. 270).

And they do so in a manifest, clearly identifiable way, which is visible in over two-thirds of the photographs of scenes constructed. Erik Erikson describes the two types of construction in the following terms:

The girl's scene is a house *interior*, represented either as a configuration of furniture without walls or by a simple *enclosure* built with blocks. In the girl's scene, people and animals are mostly *within* such an interior or enclosure, and they are primarily people or animals in a *static* (sitting or standing) position. Girls' enclosures consist of low walls only one block high, except for an occasional *elaborate doorway*. These interiors of houses, with or without walls were, for the most part, expressly *peaceful*. Often, a little girl was playing the piano. In a number of cases, however, the inside was *intruded* by animals or dangerous men. Yet the idea of an intruding creature did not necessarily lead to the defensive erection of walls or the closing of doors. Rather the majority of these intrusions have an element of humor and pleasurable excitement.

Boys' scenes are either houses with elaborate walls or façades with *protrusions* such as cones or cylinders representing ornaments or cannons. There are *high towers,* and there are entirely *exterior* scenes. In boys' constructions more people and animals are *outside* enclosures or buildings, and there are more *automotive* objects and animals *moving* along streets and intersections. There are elaborate automotive *accidents,* but there is also traffic channeled or arrested by the policeman. While high *structures* are prevalent in the configurations of the boys, there is also much play with the danger of *collapse* or downfall; *ruins* were exclusively boys' constructions. (111, pp. 270-271. Emphases in original.)

Who can fail to see that woman's tendency to be at one with the world, to internalize it, is bound up with her greater dependency on her organic universe? As an internal reflection of this connection, there is in woman, whether one likes it or not, a closer connection between mind and body than in man. The experience of maternity and the rhythms imposed by menstruation cause her belly to maintain closer ties to the emotions, and even to the intellect, than in the male. This has already been suggested by the anatomical study of the brain: in woman, there are more connections between the two cerebral hemispheres, and consequently more difficulty separating intellect and emotion. Incontestably, woman was not made to play at pure mind.

The "Fiery Mist" of Menstruation

Woman's experiences, so closely bound up with the rhythms of her belly, confirm this fact.

Strangely enough, it is among the adepts of egalitarian feminism that one finds the greatest insistence on menstruation, still a taboo subject (128, 250, 251). It is as if menstruation were *a trumpet call reminding the woman who denies herself that her body distinguishes her.* Simone de Beauvoir views menstruation as a factor in woman's "slow degradation," characterizing it in the same terms as pregnancy (she views the fetus as a "parasite" and its mother as a "laying hen" who "germinates").

Furthermore, the author of *The Second Sex* recognizes the psychological effects of menstruation. As she writes:

Nervous and irritable, a woman may be temporarily in a state of semi-lunacy; the control of the nervous centers over the peripheral and sympathetic systems is no longer assured; circulatory difficulties and certain auto-intoxications make the body seem a screen interposed between the woman and the world, a fiery mist that settles over her, stifling and cutting her off. Apprehended through this complaining and passive flesh, the whole universe seems a burden too heavy to bear. Overburdened, submerged, she becomes a stranger to herself because she is a stranger to the rest of the world. Syntheses break down, moments of time are no longer connected, other people are only recognized absentmindedly; and if reasoning and logic remain intact, as in melancholia, they are put to the service of emotional manifestations arising from a state of organic disorder. (30, p. 369)

Here, in a language somewhat reminiscent of medieval medical treatises (what are these "syntheses" that "break down"?), is a confirmation of Baudelaire's opinion: "Woman does not know how to separate her soul from her body."

Maternity: The Absolute Difference

Rooted in the world by her menstrual periods, woman is more deeply rooted in it still by the experience of maternity. Simone de Beauvoir deplores the tendency of certain mothers in this regard:

With the slightest encouragement they revive in their own cases the masculine myths: against the light of the mind they oppose the fecund darkness of Life; against the clarity of consciousness, the mysteries of inwardness; against productive liberty, the weight of this belly growing there enormously without human will. The mother-to-be feels herself one with soil and sod, stock and root; when she drowses off, her sleep is like that of brooding chaos with worlds in ferment. (30, p. 561)

The experience of maternity clearly constitutes the greatest difference between man and woman. A direct consequence of the fundamental disymmetry between the sexes (one inseminates, the other nourishes the embryo and later the child), it suffuses the life of woman. Just as in the matters of aggression or submission, gentleness or taste for competition, femininity and masculinity appear only as average tendencies around which all human variants oscillate, so here it is a question of an absolute difference. Moreover, on this subject only a woman can express the inexpressible. Listen to Florence Beaugé explain how maternity has reconciled her to "the female condition":

No man will ever see his belly undulate suddenly like a snake, will ever taste this drug of carrying a child. He could not even imagine it. How can one describe a little blow, a pinch, a hiccup? Available words are miserable, almost indecent. . . . To explain the sentiments that intoxicate a woman in these moments is as difficult as trying to define a color or an orgasm. (28)

It is wholly superfluous to give examples of mother-child attachment as a naturalist. For this is the fundamental bond, which exists everywhere and to the point of self-sacrifice. In all primate species, the females raise and protect their children, while the males play a lesser role and often even feign indifference (but is it really indifference?). Elizabeth Badinter and various others have thought that they could deny the existence of a maternal instinct. It is certainly possible to cull citations adapted to this end from history and literature. It is true that women can relegate their infants to the care of nurses, detach themselves emotionally from their children, and even practice infanticide. It is also true that there is no stereotyped behavior that is the same in all times and places and which can rightly be called "the maternal instinct." But is this to say that mother love comes *in addition,* as Elizabeth Badinter says—that it is a myth?

It is impossible to take such a notion seriously. This is, first of all, because the evidence of the emotions so clearly indicates the opposite. But it is also, and principally, because if the attachment of mothers to their children did not exist we would not even be here, so true is it that reproductive success among primates largely depends on the mother-child bond. The fact that this bond is neither systematic nor stereotyped in no way signifies its inexistence. It merely indicates that it is a character trait capable of being attenuated in certain women. Just as the anorexic lose the desire to eat, the impotent to copulate, and the depressed to live.

Maternity and Equality

The strength of the mother-child bond is so plainly evident that many feminists have reversed their positions on this subject. A major example is the sociologist Alice Rossi. In 1964, Alice Rossi called for sexual equality and demanded that men and women participate equally in child care in an identical manner (299). Today, she has reconsidered these positions and concluded that *equality does not mean doing the same thing* (300). Equality, she now feels, must be compatible with the division of the sexes in regard to child care.

Alice Rossi's point of view coincides with that of the first evolutionists, Charles Darwin and Herbert Spencer, and is no longer exceptional among feminist women. It is based on both everyday experience and a mass of biological data. For instance, a typically female hormone like oxytocin, which is involved in uterine contractions during both sex and birth, is also involved in nipple erection during nursing. From this information to regarding oxytocin as the biochemical signature of the female's aptitude for childrearing is just a short step, in Alice Rossi's view.

But is this to say that things are fixed for all eternity in this regard? Assuredly not, as the case of oxytocin itself indicates: today, a large proportion of children are no longer breastfed but bottlefed. The father can thus participate in the task without any disability. And, in fact, such participation is taking place more and more frequently—to the point that one must ask whether the use of artificial milk does not constitute a greater revolution in the sexes' relations than contraception. This example also has the merit of suggesting that biological determinisms can be modified (perhaps more so than those imposed by culture). But what does all this prove in the end? It merely shows that there is a degree of paternal interest in the child that is susceptible of being increased; but certainly not the absence between mother and child of a bond that exceeds all others by far.

Furthermore, the mother-child bond is not simply a matter of nurture and nursing. Certainly, "the human mother is," in the words of Lionel Tiger and Robin Fox, "a splendid mammal—the epitome of her order," in that she has permanent breasts (123, p. 65). But it appears that contact with the maternal body may be more important than nursing as such. This is a function of skin texture and smells. Moreover, the fact can be verified among primates. A young monkey separated from its mother is less severely traumatized if it is given a mechanical substitute that provides the impression of a relationship with a mother than if it is given milk alone. The mother supplies not only food and warmth but also attention. Moreover, recent studies confirm the greater female aptitude for detecting infantile emotions (15).

"Submissive and Imitative"

Submitted by nature to the imperatives of her hormonal and maternal lives, woman has a greater tendency than man to merge her personality with that of her loved one. Count Keyserling already perceived this very well over half a century ago. As he wrote in his book on the "Psychoanalysis of America":

> There is, nevertheless, no doubt that woman is essentially imitative, that she cedes and submits, and that, if she loves, her greatest happiness is to fuse her personality

with that of the man she loves. But here there enters precisely the consideration which demonstrates that woman is really the strong sex. She can be as submissive and imitative as one may wish: this being natural to her, she is never stymied or broken in her development. On the contrary, she has always achieved her maximum of development and perfection in giving herself to an ideal, whether god or man. This implies that man, to whatever degree he predominates, never robs woman of her intrinsic power, if only she knows her profession as woman. (185)

Obviously, such an evaluation could not be offered at present without provoking ridicule or outrage. This is because in our time the search for profundity no longer elicits anything but shrugs. Yet all the same! Let us dare to look beyond the received ideas: clearly in this relationship of the sexes it is the woman who gives herself. It is she who screams "Take me" in orgasm. Is this a stock phrase imposed by free-floating machismo? Who can truly believe it? How can one fail to see here the mark of the heart, the confession torn from the depths of the being in one of those rare moments in which it recovers, in a profoundly animal phase no doubt, the spontaneity that only rarely dares to assert itself. A piquant or rather a touching detail: the feminist movement involuntarily endorses the judgment of Count Keyserling.

The first of modern feminists, she who, with her book *The Second Sex*, threw the pebble into the pond; is she not the perfect example of the gift that the woman in love makes to the man? Not only did Simone de Beauvoir acknowledge herself to be "intellectually dominated" by Sartre, but she has described the fascination he exercised over her—to the point of drowning in humility and completely forgetting herself, as she had previously done with Zaza.

The entire life of the author of *The Second Sex* is a manifestation of the submissive and imitative behavior of the woman in love towards the loved one, who is also the admired one. In this case, imitation went so far as the renunciation of certain themes dear to Simone de Beauvoir, starting with the love of life. As for her feminist theory, it is merely the application to gender of Sartre's concept of "the Other." Thus, *in the very words with which she proclaimed the egalitarian emancipation of women, Simone de Beauvoir did homage to what for her personified the male, namely Sartre.* (207)

At this point, it is worth restating the question in a vastly more general sense. What if the neofeminist attitude, which consists in reducing the male-female difference to insignificance, were merely a means for the female of uniting still more intimately with masculine ideology? A way of submitting to the point of asking for nothing more, to the point of denying one's innermost self by merging completely with the ideology of the other? For it is indeed fundamentally this wish that appears through the demands of militant feminism: to be like men—or rather to be almost like them, for one still suspects that there is an irreducible difference somewhere, the very same that created the historical conditions for male dominance.

From this perspective, feminism is not merely, as we have already seen, machismo's partner in crime, accepting the same terms of debate and acknowledging the validity of the initial question: Is there or is there not equality? It is also an attitude fundamentally oriented toward mimickry, toward identification with the other. It is the very confession, if not of male superiority, then at least of the superiority of the male model. That is why what can be called "feminitude" must nourish itself from different sources.

12

Toward Feminitude?

Can one ever be sure of having found the truth? When dealing with a subject as entangled in ideological prejudices as that of sex differences, the question is well worth asking. Indeed, it is frequently asked by feminist writers or those claiming to be such. They regularly ask us to cast a critical eye on the sexist prejudices of those who do not think as they do. But strangely, they never apply the same critical standard to their own prejudices. Yet on the face of it, their degree of ideologization is far more evident than that of those they criticize. Still, secret prejudices may exist as well, rarely expressed yet extremely powerful. Hence the caution with which one should approach all conclusions in this area (starting, no doubt, with my own).

At the same time, if it is true there is no absolute criterion of truth, there are at least certain points of reference. Voltaire proposed one of these when he said that whenever an author, after examining a question, reaches a conclusion opposed to his convictions, it has an excellent chance of being well-founded. In the case of the female question this criterion is of interest, so striking are the confessions of certain authors.

It is the confession of Maggie Scarf, who says of her research into women and depression:

> The peculiarly high rates of depression among women cannot, in all honesty, be explained away in terms of sexist name-calling. (321, p. 554)

It is the confession of Sarah Hrdy, feminist and sociobiologist, who says:

> It was not an accident that I was drawn to the study of the Hanuman langur, a species characterized by ruthless exploitation of females by males. Rather, I suspect that I was drawn to this depressing topic by the same desire that makes victims in a

disaster who know that their situation is bad want to hear the very worst. I have sometimes compared my nine years of observation and writing about these sleek silver monkeys of India to watching a decade-long performance of a play by Strindberg, a writer who believed that males and females were as dissimilar as "two different species," and who some say went mad from dwelling too long upon the irreconcilable differences between the sexes. (157, pp. 16-17)

It is the confession of Bruce McEwen, who says of the discovery of sex differences in the human brain:

It is ironic that these studies went from the most complicated and laborious technique whereas today they are visible to the naked eye. Maybe people were afraid to look. . . . (189)

It is the confession of Evelyne Sullerot, who explains how terrified she was that she would give offense and how much she depended on the encouragement of Jacques Monod—protected, in the event, by the prestige of his Nobel Prize (351).

The conclusion is plain: nothing worthwhile is accomplished without difficulty. Many scientific conclusions were born in pain. Born against the prejudices of their authors and amid fear of exciting the hostility of the dominant intellectual milieus.

Is Feminism an Insult to Women?

And yet, when all is said and done, is there anything injurious in considering that men and women differ in many ways? To render justice to all is not to bedeck ourselves with mythical attributes but to honor real qualities. To affirm that the sexes are similar in all ways is not only to utter an absurdity but also to alienate woman, since it is she who is situated in relation to man.

The British psychologist Gleen Wilson has expressed this point very well:

What seems to have escaped the feminists is that their own position may be the biggest insult to women the gender has ever had to suffer. It assumes that women are such weak and acquiescent creatures that they can easily be induced into behaviour contrary to their inclination, and that male behaviour is some kind of ideal which they must strive to imitate.

Wilson judiciously adds:

I believe that men and women are equal in the extent to which they are predisposed by their biological nature to behave in particular ways and that the sex roles characteristically adopted by men and women in response to their differing natures are equally valuable to the species as a whole. (391)

This is the conclusion of common sense. It is also the conclusion imposed by acquaintance with the facts. For, as Evelyne Sullerot explains, "When Simone de Beauvoir said, 'One is not born, but rather becomes, a woman,' she was stating a hypothesis. But when we say today, 'One is indeed born a woman,' we are stating a fact." (351)

The Question of Otherness

One is born, but also becomes, a woman. At this stage in our analysis, having unmasked the error in the extremist aspect of de Beauvoir's ideology, I believe that, by the same token, we should not deprive ourselves of its potentially fruitful aspects. For though it is false to deny the original difference, false to say "One is not born a woman," it would be a mistake to conclude from this that the second part of the famous sentence of *The Second Sex* is necessarily false as well. One may be surprised to see me espousing such a viewpoint, but I believe that, paradoxically, although it starts from a false premise, the second part of the sentence is accurate. In my view, the question of otherness, the center of Simone de Beauvoir's concerns, is a legitimate one. *The Second Sex* hypertrophies it but did not create it. Woman is the Other. She is woman because she is seen as such by man. Otherness is a fundamental category of human thought, as indicated by such oppositions as good and evil, day and night, sun and moon, etc. But in the case of sex differences, there is a fundamental dissymmetry. The word man designates both the human species and the male, whereas the word woman is restricted to gender. All works on sex differences (starting, no doubt, with the present one) situate woman in relation to man—not the reverse.

For the male is indeed the point of reference. Insidiously, this criterion permeates the most minor details of social life. In this regard, a remark by Simone de Beauvoir appears to me to be highly significant. She was sometimes told by men that "You think thus and so because you are a woman." She could only reply, "I think thus and so because it is true"; not, "And you think the contrary because you are a man" (30, p. xviii). Seemingly, *woman is the Other of man; yet she does not view man as her own Other*. No doubt one should qualify this judgment (like all those of Simone de Beauvoir): let us say, rather, that one of the partners regards the other more as his Other. Woman thus participates in the dissymmetry. Furthermore, studies of adolescent psychology indicate the existence of a tendency among girls to underrate themselves. Unlike boys, who attribute a superiority to their own sex, girls often believe it is better to be a boy. Many girls dissociate themselves from their peers, affirming that they do not resemble the type specimen of their own sex as they themselves describe it (375, 399).

Not only is there an absence of reciprocity in this regard but, in the case of man and woman, the form of otherness is completely different from that which exists in other situations of oppression. Thus, for slaves or proletarians, there was a *before* to which the individual can refer in his demands. Nothing comparable exists in the case of women. In this case, otherness appears as an absolute. Moreover, women live dispersed among men and lack the capacity to reject them. "The proletariat," writes Simone de Beauvoir, "can propose to massacre the ruling class, and a fanatical Jew or Negro might dream of getting sole possession of the atom bomb and making humanity wholly Jewish or black; but women cannot even dream of exterminating the males." That is because in this case there is a biological given. "Here is to be found the basic trait of woman: she is the Other in a totality of which the two components are necessary to one another" (30, pp. xxii-xxiii).

Maintained in a state of inferiority in relation to man, woman is indeed inferior in this schema. The verb *to be* refers here to a *become being,* not to something that is necessarily immutable. But sexism uses female inferiorization to establish female inferiority and hence to legitimate woman's status as natural. For de Beauvoir, the biological difference, however natural it may be, is only the first step in this process, not its justification. As she writes:

> Thus we must view the facts of biology in the light of an ontological, economic, social, and psychological context. The enslavement of the female to the species and the limitations of her various powers are extremely important facts; the body of woman is one of the essential elements in her situation in the world. But that body is not enough to define her as woman; there is no true living reality except as manifested by the conscious individual through activities and in the bosom of a society. Biology is not enough to give an answer to the question that is before us: why is woman the *Other?* Our task is to discover how the nature of woman has been affected throughout the course of history; we are concerned to find out what humanity has made of the human female. (30, p. 41)

At the risk of surprising some, I do not hesitate to concur with this opinion. I willingly agree with Simone de Beauvoir that one becomes, more than one is born, a woman. But I also consider that *scientific analysis in no way authorizes one to oppose becoming to being born.* "One is not born, but rather becomes, a woman," writes the author of *The Second Sex* (30, p. 301). In this famous sentence, the premise is incorrect but the conclusion is accurate. Having taken the measure of the original difference, one should attempt to understand its significance. It is not a question of interpreting it as an absolute difference that freezes behavior in a manner so stereotyped as to deprive the individual of all control over his destiny. The original difference is real, but in a sense it is without interest: what matters is the significance it receives from its actualization. As a potential that encounters the conditions of familial, social, cultural, and other environments, the difference is progressively charged with meaning. It leads to identification. The little boy and little girl receive their sexual labels—as, indeed, they receive a variety of other labels: social (rich, poor), racial (white, black, yellow), academic (good student, dunce); and as later on they will receive still others: political (left, right), professional, etc.

Though it comes from outside the individual, the labeling is not thereby independent of him. Its purpose is to situate him, to give meaning to what he is. It is a means of establishing that a destiny is unfolding and a human condition is being assumed. The important thing is indeed the significance we assign to the differences and not the differences themselves. But does the significance erase the differences? Why do we presume that there must be a disjunction or an antagonism between the two? In my view, this is the heart of the matter.

Of course, de Beauvoir would have no difficulty replying that the problem with sexism is that, as the Other, woman lacks complete freedom. To the author of *The Second Sex*, let us recall, the goal cannot be to seek happiness; it is instead freedom, conceptualized from the perspective of "existential morality":

> Every subject plays his part as such specifically through exploits or projects that serve as a mode of transcendence; he achieves liberty only through a continual reaching out toward other liberties. There is no justification for present existence other than its expansion into an indefinitely open future. Every time transcendence falls back into immanence, stagnation, there is a degradation of existence into the *"en-soi"*—the brutish life of subjection to given conditions—and of liberty into constraint and contingence. This downfall represents a moral fault if the subject

consents to it; if it is inflicted upon him, it spells frustration and oppression. In both cases it is an absolute evil. Every individual concerned to justify his existence feels that his existence involves an undefined need to transcend himself, to engage in freely chosen projects. Now, what peculiarly signalizes the situation of woman is that she—a free and autonomous being like all human creatures—nevertheless finds herself living in a world where men compel her to assume the status of the Other. They propose to stabilize her as object and to doom her to immanence since her transcendence is to be overshadowed and forever transcended by another ego which is essential and sovereign. The drama of woman lies in this conflict between the fundamental aspirations of every subject—who always regards the self as essential—and the compulsions of a situation in which she is the inessential. (30, p. 31)

But is the woman who assumes her femininity removed from transcendence? Why must she deny her sex to affirm herself as an individual? Why must she cut out part of herself to become herself? Why must her more imitative nature be viewed as a rejection of freedom? Why should it not reveal itself instead to be the mark of an authentic destiny? From childhood on, the girl is more sociable, more smiling, more interested in joining groups of adults, in inserting herself into a social space, while the boy more often joins a group of his playmates or more willingly isolates himself, producing in his corner the design of a construction of the external universe. After all, why must the fact of being oriented toward others, toward imitation, toward the construction of the internal universe, be devalidating? One can be influenced by great thinkers without losing one's soul. Simone de Beauvoir acknowledges this herself and her entire lifetime of devotion to Sartre bears witness to it. Perhaps she would have produced a superior literary output without this suffocating frequentation. But perhaps not. In my view, it is still seeing things too much through the distorting lens of the machismo-antisexism dichotomy to attribute transcendence solely to masculine behaviors that reject submission and imitation. That is why I do not think that sexual labeling or the otherness dear to de Beauvoir implies artificiality or inauthenticity.

The individual's immersion in the social context must no longer be seen as antagonistic to biological determinism. It does not work against heredity. On the contrary, it arrives to complement an original determinism as its mirror and reflection. Or, if one prefers, as its amplifier.

This point of view carries us far beyond the usual alternative of biological/social, nature/nurture or genetic/cultural—a dichotomy that is permanently trapped in a vicious circle. It is true that it is almost always women who care for children—a universal trait that evokes a biological imperative; but it is also true that women are socially encouraged to do so—which pleads in favor of social determinism; it is true that little girls are more feminine and little boys more masculine, but also that they are socialized to be that way; that men generally tend to dominate women, but also that tradition places women in less domineering roles.

To escape this vicious circle, we must go beyond the mere observation of differences and confront the evidence as a whole. Here sociological analysis and traditional sexology, viewed in isolation, reveal themselves to be singularly impoverished. One must bring together the evidence of embryology, genetics, ethology, primatology, evolutionary theory, endocrinology, neurophysiology, ethnology, etc. Only by taking a journey through all of these disciplines, as we have done in the course of these pages, can we unscramble the plot—and that, despite many gaps in our knowledge, with a most remarkable degree of coherence.

Let us resume the overall schema and thereby consolidate the knowledge we have acquired. It all begins with one small genetic difference, which in mammals is represented by the presence of a Y chromosome in the male. From this initial difference, an embryological sequence unfolds in which the fetus is masculinized by male hormones if it has a Y chromosome, or remains female if it has a second X chromosome. In the first case, it produces a male, who will possess a multitude of missiles limited to the role of chromosome carriers; in the second case, it produces a female, whose large eggs are destined to nourish embryos. Armed with his external apparatus and bullets, the male will be oriented toward conquest, penetration, parading, and aggression, while the female will be oriented toward receptivity, choice, and quality. From this point onward, two types of strategies proceed to elaborate themselves, in terms of sexuality—the male will be more dispersed and the female more monogamous—but also in terms of intellect. Confounding conquest and comprehension, the male will envision science as a break with the world, as abstraction or dissection, while the female will construct knowledge in collusion with the world and with respect for its harmony. Psychology indicates this, neurophysiology confirms it while explaining it, and the history of science documents its effects on the evolution of knowledge.

Thus all the main evidence fits together. It persuades by its extensiveness, but even more by its coherence.

The Rise of Woman or the Fall of Man?

Is this to say that everything is locked into a biological determinism from which there is no escape? Assuredly not. Biological does not mean immutable.

Furthermore, relations between the sexes have undergone a manifest evolution. From the demands of feminists to the creation of cabinet-level departments of women, and passing by what are doubtless more significant developments like unisex fashions or the participation of both parents in infant care, our time has witnessed numerous changes.

Still more characteristically, many aspects of relations between the sexes are tending toward equalization—even though, as we have noted, what people think has changed much less than what they say. Man is becoming feminized and woman is becoming masculinized.

In many cases, such changes do not go beyond surface appearances or demagogy. Yet, as a general phenomenon, the feminization of the world appears to be real enough. How, then, are we to interpret it in light of the facts just presented?

As we have noted, the existence of social changes is in no way antagonistic to biological determinism, which only represents a set of predispositions that are capable of actualizing themselves or not as a function of context. The problem here is to understand how all this could have come about. If what we have said concerning the essence of the male-female relationship is correct, then the original element must have been the abandonment of masculinity more than the rise of femininity, since the latter affirms itself in relationship to man and not the reverse. Logically, this abandonment must have made it impossible to be admired for one's femininity. Simultaneously, a gap appeared that demanded to be filled. When the father defaults in his functions, whether through death or a forfeiture resulting from illness or alcoholism, the wife commonly takes charge and assumes the duties of a head of household. Similarly, the wife of a deceased monarch often assumes the direction of a kingdom's affairs. From this standpoint, it was inevitable that the feminization of the human male, rejecting his sense of responsibility with all that it implies of risk and arbitrariness, should have led to homogenization—that is to say, among other things, to the masculinization of women.

Here one doubtless encounters a concrete manifestation of the transcendent. A woman only realizes herself as a woman in the presence of a man who plays the role of a man. In the same way, a teacher only becomes himself in front of his students, an actor in front of his audience, and a general in front of his troops. The actualization of one competence requires its relationship to another.

To Be Something Instead of Nothing

This reciprocal realization through the resonance of different but complementary aptitudes appears to be not only logical but alone capable of conferring value. Consider, in this regard, the feminism of the 1960s. As Arianna Stassinopoulos has written, in the final analysis the majority of feminists "cannot decide whether they want to become men or destroy them" (349, p. 136). In reality, it appears that they want to do both at once. This is not only contradictory but self-destructive. To devalidate the partner one seeks to emulate is to devalidate oneself.

That is why it is necessary to go *beyond feminism,* brittle and bitter, in order to *advocate feminitude*, based on a recognition of the values proper to each sex, which has nothing to fear from the affirmation of its own identity. That is why the study of the differences between the sexes, and still more of their differing relationships, is of such central importance. It highlights those things that allow one truly to be oneself. It is, therefore, not at all a matter of realizing a catalogue for a biologist; after all, there are at least as many similarities as differences between the sexes. Moreover, from the genetic standpoint, what approaches the sexes is much more apparent than what separates them (one chromosome out of 46!). It is a matter, instead, of clarifying the meaning of the differences. These must no longer be interpreted as the mark of some ancient curse or of a primordial inferiority. On the contrary, by consenting to examine sex differences in the full light of day, they become validating for both sexes. They originalize. Better still, they are one of the marks of destiny. They bear witness to the fact that every human being is something instead of nothing.

Bibliography

1. Albistur, M., and Armogathe, E. *Histoire du féminisme français*. 2 vols. Paris: Editions des femmes, 1977.
2. Alexander, R. *Darwinism and Human Affairs*. Seattle, Wash.: University of Washington Press/Pitman, 1980.
3. Allen, D.E. The Women Members of the Botanical Society of London, 1836–1856. *British Journal for the History of Science* 13 (1980):240–254.
4. Amram, F. The Innovative Woman. *New Scientist* 102 (24 May 1984):10–12.
5. Andersson, M. Female Choice Selects for Extreme Tail Length in a Widowbird. *Nature* 299 (1982):818–820.
6. *Annales de démographie historique: Démographie historique et condition féminine*. Paris: Mouton, 1982.
7. Arai, Y. Synaptic Correlates of Sexual Differentiation. *Trends in Neuroscience* 4 (1981):291–293.
8. Archer, J., and Westeman K. Sex Differences in the Aggressive Behaviour of Schoolchildren. *British Journal of Social Psychology* 20 (1981):31–36.
9. Arditti, R.; Brennan, P.; and Cavrak, S.; eds. *Science and Liberation*. Boston: South End Press, 1970.
10. Arendash, G.W., and Gorsk, R.A. Enhancement of Sexual Behavior in Female Rats by Neonatal Transplantation of Brain Tissue from Males. *Science* 217 (1982):1276–1278.
11. Arnold, A.P. Model Systems for the Study of Sexual Differentiation of the Nervous System. *Trends in Pharmacological Science* 2 (1981):148–149.
12. Arnold, A.P., and Saltiel A. Sexual Difference in Pattern Hormone Accumulation in the Brain of a Songbird. *Science* 205(1979): 702–705.
13. Attekar, A.S. *The Position of Women in Hindu Civilisation*. Benares: Motohal Banarsidas, 1956.
14. Austin, C.R., and Edwards, R.G., eds. *Mechanisms of Sex Differentiation in Animals and Man*. London and New York: Academic Press, 1981.
15. Babchuk, W.A.; Hames, R.B.; and Thompson, R.A. Sex Differences in the Recognition of Infant Facial Expressions of Emotion: The Primary Caretaker Hypothesis. *Ethology and Sociobiology* 6 (1985):89–101.

16. Badinter, E. *L'amour en plus*. Paris: Flammarion, 1980.
17. ————. *Emilie, Emilie, l'ambition féminine au XVIIIe siècle*. Paris: Flammarion, 1983.
18. Baldwin, R.O. Stability of Masculinity–Femininity Scores over an Eleven-Year Period. *Sex Roles* 10 (1984):257–260.
19. Barash, D. *Sociobiology and Behavior*. London: Heinemann, 1977.
20. ————. *The Whisperings Within: Evolution and the Origin of Human Nature*. New York: Harper and Row, 1979.
21. Barbach, L. *Women Discover Orgasm: A Therapist's Guide to a New Treatment Approach*. New York: Free Press, 1980.
22. Bardeche, M. *Histoire des femmes*. 2 vols. Paris: Stock, 1968.
23. Bardin, C.W., and Catterhall, J.F. Testosterone: A Major Determinant of Extragenital Sexual Dimorphism. *Science* 211 (1981):1285–1294.
24. Baron, A.S. Selection, Development and Socialization of Women. *Business Quarterly* 42 (1977):61.
25. Baron, M. Polarity and Sex Effect in Genetic Transmission of Affective Disorders. *Human Heredity* 33 (1983):112–118.
26. Baron, M.G. L'informatique fait-elle peur aux filles? *Figaro,* 6 February 1985.
27. Bateson, P., ed. *Mate Choice*. Cambridge: Cambridge University Press, 1983.
28. Beaugé, F. Alors, c'est ça l'amour maternel? *Le Monde*, 19–20 February 1978.
29. Beaumont-Maillet, L. *La guerre des sexes*. Paris: Albin Michel, 1984.
30. Beauvoir, S. de. *The Second Sex*. Translated by H.M. Parshley. New York: Knopf, 1953. (Orig. French ed. 1949.)
31. Beckwith, J., and Durkin, J. Girls, Boys and Math. *Science for the People* 13 (1981):6–35.
32. Bell, G. *The Masterpiece of Nature: The Evolution and Genetics of Sexuality*. Berkeley: University of California Press, 1982.
33. Belotti, E.G. *Du côté des petites filles*. Paris: Editions des femmes, 1974.
34. Benbow, C.P., and Stanley, J.C. Sex Differences in Mathematical Ability: Fact or Artifact? *Science* 210 (1980):1262–1264.
35. ————. Mathematical Ability: Is Sex a Factor? *Science* 212 (1981):118–119.
36. ————. Sex Differences in Mathematical Reasoning Ability: More Facts. *Science* 222 (1983):1029–1031.
37. Bernardin, H.J., ed. *Women in the Work Force*. New York: Praeger, 1982.
38. Bingham, R. Symons Says: Sex is Something that Women Have and Men Want. *Science 83* IV (January-February 1983):66–71.
39. Birnbaum, M.H. Relationships among Models of Salary Bias. *American Psychologist* 40 (1985):862–866.
40. Bischof, N. De la signification biologique du bisexualisme. In *Le fait féminin*, edited by E. Sullerot, 34–50. Paris: Fayard, 1978.

41. Black, N. and Cottrell, A.B., eds. *Women and World Change: Equity Issues in Development.* Beverly Hills: Sage, 1981.

42. Blatter, P. Sex Differences in Spatial Ability: The X-Linked Gene Theory. *Perceptual and Motor Skills* 55 (1982):455–462.

43. Bleier, R. *Science and Gender: A Critique of Biology and its Theories on Women.* Oxford: Pergamon, 1984.

44. Blume, E. Un lien entre dépression et syndromes prémenstruales? JAMA (French ed.) 8 (1983):90–92.

45. Blunden, K. *Le travail et la vertu.* Paris: Payot, 1982.

46. Blurton Jones, N.G., and Konner, M.J. Sex Differences in Behaviour of London and Bushman Children. In *Comparative Ecology and Behaviour of Primates*, edited by R.P. Michael and J.H. Crook, 689–750. London: Academic Press, 1973.

47. Blute, M. The Sociobiology of Sex and Sexes Today. *Current Anthropology* 25 (1984):193–212.

48. Bock, R.D. and Kolakowski, D. Further Evidence of Sex-Linked Major-Gene Influence on Human Spatial Visualizing Ability. *American Journal of Human Genetics* 25 (1973):1–14.

49. Boesch, C. and Boesch, H. Sex Differences in the Use of Natural Hammers by Wild Chimpanzees: A Preliminary Report. *Journal of Human Evolution* 10 (1981):585–593.

50. Boles, D.B. X-Linkage of Spatial Ability: A Critical Review. *Child Development* 51 (1980):625–635.

51. Bouthoul, G. *Sociologie de la politique.* 4th ed. Paris: Presses Universitaires de France/Collection Que sais-je?, 1977.

52. Bower, B. The Left Hand of Math and Verbal Talent. *Science News* 127 (27 April 1985):p. 263.

53. Breedlove, S.M. Hormone Accumulation in a Sexually Dimorphic Motor Nucleus of the Rat Spinal Cord. *Science* 210 (1980):564–566.

54. Brighton Women and Science Group: *Alice Through the Microscope.* London: Virago, 1980.

55. Brissaud, P. Rattraper les hommes? *Tribune Médicale*, 21 April 1984, 24–28.

56. Broverman, I.K.; Vogel, S.R.; Broverman, D.M.; Clarkson, F.E.; and Rosenkrantz, P.S. Sex Role Stereotypes: A Current Appraisal. *Journal of Social Issues* 28 (1972):59–79.

57. Brownmiller, S. *Against Our Will: Men, Women and Rape.* New York: Simon and Schuster, 1975.

58. Bruer, J.T. Women in Science: Lack of Full Participation. *Science* 21 (1983):p. 1339.

59. Brush, L.R.; Char, C.; Irwin, N.; and Takata, G. *Encouraging Girls in Mathematics: The Problem and the Solution.* Cambridge, Mass. Abt Books, 1980.

60. Bullivant, S. U.S. Women Break into Engineering. *New Scientist* 95 (30 September 1982):918–921.

61. Calder-Marshall, A. *The Sage of Sex.* New York: Putnam, 1959.

62. Calverton, V.F., and Schmalhausen, S.D., eds. *Sex in Civilization.* New York: Garden City, 1929.
63. Cassell, J. *A Group Called Women: Sisterhood and Symbolism in the Feminist Movement.* 1977.
64. Cattell, J.M. A Statistical Study of Eminent Men. *Popular Science Monthly* 62 (1903):359–377.
65. Chagnon, N. Yanomamö Social Organization and Warfare. In *War: The Anthropology of Armed Conflict and Aggression,* edited by M. Fried, M. Harris, and R. Murphy. New York: Natural History Press, 1968.
66. Charnov, E.I. *The Theory of Sex Allocation.* London: Princeton University Press, 1982.
67. Charvet, J. *Feminism.* London: Dent, 1982.
68. Chipman, S. Mathematical Ability: Is Sex a Factor? *Science* 212 (1981):114–115.
69. Christen, Y. *L'heure de la sociobiologie.* Paris: Albin Michel, 1979.
70. ———. *Le grand affrontement: Marx et Darwin.* Paris: Albin Michel, 1981.
71. ———. *Le dossier Darwin.* Paris: Copernic, 1982.
72. ———. *Biologie de l'idéologie.* Paris: Carrere-J.J. Pauvert, 1985.
73. ———. *L'homme bioculturel.* Paris: Le Rocher, 1986.
74. Christian, B. *Black Feminist Criticism: Perspectives on Black Women Writers.* Oxford: Pergamon, 1985.
75. Cliquet, R.L. The Relevance of Sociobiological Theory for Emancipatory Feminism. *Journal of Human Evolution* 13 (1984):117–127.
76. Cohen, P.S. Sex, Gender and Equality: Or, The Conversion of Melford E. Spiro. *British Journal of Sociology* 32 (1981):411–431.
77. Cole, J.R. *Fair Science: Women in the Scientific Community.* New York: Free Press, 1979.
78. ———. Women in Science. *American Scientist* 69 (1981):385–391.
79. Comfort, A. *Sex in History.* New York: Stein and Day, 1980.
80. Crabbe, B.; Delfosse, M.-L.; Gaiardo, L.; Verlaeckt, G.; and Wilwerth, E. *Les femmes dans les livres scolaires.* Bruxelles: Pierre Mardage, 1985.
81. Crachat, C: *Le sexisme ordinaire.* Paris: Le Seuil.
82. Daly, M., and Wilson, M. *Sex, Evolution and Behavior,* North Scituate, Mass.: Duxbury Press, 1978.
83. Darwin, C. *De l'origine des espèces par sélection naturelle ou des lois de transformation des êtres organisés.* Translated by C. Royer. 2 vols. Paris: Flammarion, 1862. (Orig. English ed. 1859.)
84. ———. *La descendance de l'homme et la sélection sexuelle.* Paris: Reinwald, n.d. Translated by E. Barbier from the second English ed., 1874. (Orig. English ed. 1871.)
85. Davis, A. *Femmes, race et classe.* Paris: Des femmes, 1983. Translated by D. Taffin and the Des Femmes collective. (Orig. ed. 1981.)
86. Dawkins, R. *Le gène égoiste.* Paris: Menges, 1978. Translated by J.

Pavesti and N. Chaptal. (Orig. ed. 1976.)

87. Dearden, J. Sex Linked Differences of Political Behavior: An Investigation of Their Possible Primate Origins. *Social Sciences Information* 13 (1974):19–45.

88. Deaux, K. *The Behavior of Women and Men.* Monterey, Calif.: Brooks-Cole, 1976.

89. Deutsch, H. *La psychologie des femmes.* Translated by Benoit. 2 vols. Paris: Presses Universitaires de France, 1949.

90. De Visscher, P. *Attitudes antiféministes et milieux intellectuels.* Louvain and Paris: Nauwelaerts, 1956.

91. De Vries, G.J.; De Bruin, J.P.C.; Uylings, H.B.M; and Corner, M.A. *Sex Differences in the Brain: Relation Between Structure and Function.* New York: Elsevier, 1984.

92. Doverspike, D.; Cellar, D.; Barrett, G.V.; and Alexander, R. Sex Differences in Short-Term Memory Processsing. *Perceptual and Motor Skills* 58 (1984):135–139.

93. Draper, P. Social and Economic Constraints on Child Life among the !Kung. In *Kalahari Hunter-Gatherers: Studies of the !Kung San and their Neighbors*, edited by R.B. Lee and I. De Vore. Cambridge, Mass.: Harvard University Press, 1976.

94. Duverger, M. *The Political Role of Women.* Paris: Unesco, 1955.

95. Dyer, K.F. Catching Up the Men. *New Scientist* 103 (2 August 1984):25–26.

96. Easlea, B. *Science and Sexual Oppression: Patriarchy's Confrontation with Woman and Nature.* London: Weidenfeld and Nicolson, 1981.

97. Easlea, B. *Fathering the Unthinkable: Masculinity, Scientists and the Nuclear Arms Race.* Pluto Press, 1984.

98. Eaubonne, F. d': *Le complexe de Diane.* Paris: Julliard, 1951.

99. ———: *Y a-t-il encore des hommes.* Paris: Flammarion, 1964.

100 ———: *Le féminisme.* Paris, Alain Moreau, 1972.

101. Edgell, S. *Middle Class Couples: A Study of Segregation, Domination and Inequality in Marriage.* London: George Allen and Unwin, 1980.

102. Egelman, E.; Alper, J.; Leibowitz, L.; Beckwith, J.; Levine, R.; and Leeds, A. Mathematical Ability: Is Sex a Factor? *Science* 212 (1981): p. 115.

103. Ehrhardt, A.A., and Meyer-Bahlburg, H.F.L. Effects of Prenatal Sex Hormones on Gender-Related Behavior. *Science* 211 (1981):1312–1318.

104. Eisenberg, L. La répartition différentielle des troubles psychologiques selon le sexe. In *Le fait féminin*, edited by E. Sullerot, 313–331. Paris: Fayard, 1978.

105. Elderton, E.M. *A First Study of the Influence of Parental Alcoholism on the Physique and Ability of the Offspring.* London, 1910.

106. Ellis, H. *A Study of British Genius.* London: Hurst-Blackett, 1904.

107 ———. *Etudes de psychologie sexuelle.* Translated by Van Gennep. 19 vols. Paris: Mercure de France, 1921–1936.

108. Ellis, L. Developmental Androgen Fluctuations and the Fixed Dimensions of Mammalian Sex (With Emphasis upon the Behavioral Dimension and the Human Species). *Ethology and Sociobiology* 3 (1982):171–197.

109. El-Saadaoui, N. *La face cachée d'Eve.* Paris: Des femmes, 1982.

110. El Saadawi, N. *Woman at Point Zero.* London: Zed Press, 1983.

111. Erikson, E. *Identity: Youth and Crisis.* New York: Norton, 1968.

112. Escoffier-Lambiotte, C. Le sexe du cerveau. *Le Monde,* 3 November 1982.

113. Eysenck, H.J., and Wilson, G.D. *The Psychology of Sex.* London: Dent, 1979.

114. Fee, E. A Feminist Critique of Scientific Objectivity. *Science for the People* 14 (1982):5–8, 30.

115. ———, ed. *Women and Health: The Politics of Sex in Medicine.* Bajwood, 1982.

116. Ferry, G. How Women Figure in Science. *New Scientist,* 1 April 1982, 94:10–13.

117. ———. Was Wise Worthwhile? *New Scientist* 105 (3 January 1985):28–31.

118. ———, and Moore J. True Confessions of Women in Science. *New Scientist* 95 (1 July 1982):27–30.

119. Fischette, C.T.; Biegon, A.; and McEwen, B.S. Sex Differences in Serotonin 1 Receptor Binding in Rat Brain. *Science* 222 (1983):333–335.

120. Fisher, H.E. *La stratégie du sexe.* Translated by C. Cassin. Paris: Calmann-Levy, 1983. (Orig. ed. 1982.)

121. Fisher, S. The Female Orgasm: *Psychology, Physiology, Fantasy.* New York: Basic Books, 1973.

122. Fox, L.H.; Brody, L.; and Tobin, D.; eds. *Women and Mathematical Mystique.* Baltimore: Johns Hopkins, 1980.

123. Fox, R., and Tiger, L. *The Imperial Animal.* New York: Holt, 1971.

124. Fraisse, G. *Clémence Royer, philosophe et femme de science.* Paris: La découverte, 1985.

125. Freeman, J. *The Politics of Women's Liberation: A Case Study of an Emerging Social Movement and its Relation to the Policy Process.* 1977.

126. Friedan, B. *The Feminine Mystique.* New York: Norton, 1963.

127. ———. *The Second Stage.* New York: Summit Books, 1981.

128. Friedman, R.C., ed. *Behavior and the Menstrual Cycle.* New York: Marcel Dekker, 1982.

129. Garfield, E. Why Aren't There More Women in Science? *Current Contents,* 26 April 1982, 5–12.

130. Gaudio, A., and Pelletier, R. *Femmes d'Islam ou le sexe interdit.* Paris: Denoël-Gonthier, 1980.

131. Geschwind, N., and Behan, P. Left-Handedness: Association with Immune Disease, Migraine, and Developmental Learning Disorder.

Proceedings of the National Academy of Sciences 79 (1982):5097–5100.

132. Ghiselin, M.T. *The Economy of Nature and the Evolution of Sex.* Berkeley: University of California Press, 1974.

133. Gluckksmann, A. *Sexual Dimorphism in Human and Mammalian Biology and Pathology.* London and New York: Academic Press, 1981.

134. Goldberg, S. *The Inevitability of Patriarchy.* Rev. ed. London: Temple Smith, 1977. (Orig. ed. 1973.)

135. Gordon, L. *Woman's Body, Woman's Right: A Social History of Birth Control in America.* Viking Press, 1976.

136. Gordon, L. Birth Control and the Eugenists. *Science for the People* 9 (March-April 1977):8–15.

137. Goy, R.W., and McEwen, B.S., eds. *Sexual Differentiation of the Brain.* Cambridge, Mass.: MIT Press, 1980.

138. Greer, G. *Sex and Destiny: The Politics of Human Fertility.* New York: Harper and Row, 1984.

139. Gribbin, M. Boys Muscle in on the Keyboard. *New Scientist* 103 (30 August 1984):16–17.

140. Gualteri, T., and Hicks, R.E. An Immunoreactive Theory of Selective Male Affliction. *The Behavioral and Brain Sciences* 8 (1985):379–394.

141. Gur, R.C.; Gur, R.E.; Obrist, W.D.; Hungerbuhler, J.P.; Younkin, D.; Rosen, A.D.; Skolnick, B.E.; and Reivich, M. Sex and Handedness Differences in Cerebral Blood Flow During Rest and Cognitive Activity. *Science* 217 (1982):659–661.

142. Halimi, G. *La cause des femmes.* Paris: Grasset, 1974.

143. Hamilton, J.B., and Mestler, G.E. Mortality and Survival Comparison of Eunuchs with Intact Men and Women in a Mentally Retarded Population. *Journal of Gerontology* 24 (1969):395–411.

144. Harding, J. How the World Attracts Girls to Science. *New Scientist* 99 (15 September 1983):754–755.

145. Harding, S., and Hintikka, M., eds. *Discovering Reality.* Dordrecht and London: Reidel, 1983.

146. Harlan, R.E.; Gordon, J.H.; and Gorski, R.A. Sexual Differentiation of the Brain: Implications for Neuroscience. *Reviews of Neuroscience* 4 (1979):31–32.

147. Harris, L.J. Sex Differences in Spatial Ability: Possible Environmental, Genetic and Neurological Factors. In *Asymmetrical Function of the Brain*, edited by M. Kinsbourne, 415–522. Cambridge: Cambridge University Press, 1980.

148. Hartsock, N.C.M. *Money, Sex and Power: Toward a Feminist Historical Materialism.* New York: Longman, 1983.

149. Hebert, M. *Ainsi disent-elles.* Paris: Opuscule-Garnier, 1982.

150. Henriques, N. Women In Computing: Escape from the Female Ghetto. *New Scientist* 103 (9 August 1984):17–19.

151. Herbert, W. Premenstrual Changes. *Science News* 122 (1982):380–381.

152. Herbert, W. Curing Femininity. *Science News* 124 (1983):170–171.

153. Heymans, G. *La psychologie des femmes*. Translated by Le Senne. Paris: Alcan, 1925. (Orig. ed. 1910.)

154. Hier, D.B., and Crowley, W.F. Spatial Ability in Androgen-Deficient Men. *New England Journal of Medicine* 306 (1982):1202–1205.

155. Hoyenga, K.B., and Hoyenga, K.T. *Sex Differences: Psychological, Cultural and Biological Issues*. Boston and Toronto: Little Brown, 1979.

156. Hrdy, S.B. Heat Loss: The Absence of Estrus Reflects a Change in Sexual Strategy. *Science 83* IV (October 1983):73–78.

157. ———. *The Woman That Never Evolved*. Cambridge, Mass.: Harvard University Press, 1981.

158. Hubbard, R.; Henifin, M.S.; and Fried, B.; eds. *Women Look at Biology Looking at Women: A Collection of Feminist Critiques*. Cambridge, Mass.: Schenkman, 1979.

159. ———. *Biological Woman: The Convenient Myth: A Collection of Feminist Essays and a Comprehensive Bibliography*. Cambridge, Mass.: Schenkman, 1982.

160. Hubbard, R., and Lowe, M., eds. *Genes and Gender II: Pitfalls in Research on Sex and Gender*. New York: Gordian Press, 1979.

161. Humphreys, S.M., ed. *Women and Minorities in Science*. Boulder, Colo.: Westview Press, 1982.

162. Hyde, J.S. How Large are Cognitive Gender Differences? *American Psychologist* 36 (1981):892–901.

163. Imperato-McGinley, J.; Peterson, R.E.; and Gautier, T. Gender Identity and Hermaphroditism. *Science* 191 (1976):p. 872.

164. Imperato-McGinley, J. Androgens and the Evolution of Male-Gender Identity. *New England Journal of Medicine* 300 (1979):1233–1237.

165. Inglis, J., and Lawson, J.S. Sex Differences in the Effects of Unilateral Brain Damage on Intelligence. *Science* 212 (1981):693–695.

166. Inglis, J.; Ruckman, M.; Lawson, J. S.; MacLean, A. W.; and Monga, T. N. Sex Differences in the Cognitive Effects of Unilateral Brain Damage: Comparison of Stroke Patients and Normal Control Subjects. *Cortex* 19 (1983):551–555.

167. Jackson, M. Sex Research and the Construction of Sexuality: A Tool of Male Supremacy? *Women's Studies International Forum* 7 (1984):43–51.

168. Jaeger, G.A. *Les femmes d'abordage*. Paris: Clancier-Guénaud, 1984.

169. Jahoda, G. Sex and Ethnic Differences on a Spatial-Perceptual Task: Some Hypotheses Tested. *British Journal of Psychology* 71 (1980):425–431.

170. Janssen-Jurreit, M.-L. *Sexism: The Male Monopoly on History and Thought*. Translated by V. Moberg. New York: Farrar, Straus and Giroux, 1982. (Orig. ed. 1976.)

171. Jarvik, L.F. Human Intelligence: Sex Differences. *Acta Geneticae Medicae et Gemellologiae* 24 (1975):189–211.

172. Jensen, A.R. *Bias in Mental Testing*. London: Methuen, 1980.

173. ———, and Reynolds, C.R. Sex Differences on the WISC-R. *Personality and Individual Differences* 4 (1983):223–226.
174. Johnson, O., and Harley, C. Handedness and Sex Differences in Cognitive Tests of Brain Laterality. *Cortex* 16 (1980):73–82.
175. Joran, T. *Autour du féminisme*. Paris, 1906.
176. Jost, A. Le développement sexuel prénatal. In *Le fait féminin*, edited by E. Sullerot, 85–90. Paris: Fayard, 1978.
177. *Journal of Psychiatric Education*: Towards the New Psychology of Women and Men. *Journal of Psychiatric Education* 7 (Spring 1983): p. 80.
178. Justice, B., and Pore, R., eds. *Toward the Second Decade: The Impact of the Women's Movement on American Institutions*. Westport, Conn.: Greenwood Press, 1981.
179. Kaplan, M. A Woman's View of DSM III. *American Psychologist* 38 (1983):786–792.
180. Kaufmann-McCall, D. Politics of Difference: The Women's Movement in France from May 1968 to Mitterand. *Journal of Women in Culture and Society* 9 (1983):282–293.
181. Keller, E.F. *Reflections on Gender and Science*. New Haven: Yale University Press, 1985.
182. Kelly, A. Mathematical Ability: Is Sex a Factor? *Science* 212 (1981): p. 117.
183. ———. Why Girls Don't Do Science. *New Scientist* 94 (20 May 1982):497–500.
184. Kernbaum, S.; Tazi, L.; and Champagne D. Sexe et maladies infectieuses. *Bulletin de l'Institut Pasteur* 74 (1976):359–382.
185. Keyserling, H. de: *Psychanalyse de l'Amérique*. Paris: Stock, 1930.
186. Kinsey, A.C.; Pomeroy, W.B.; Martin, C.E.; and Gebhard, P.H. *Sexual Behavior in the Human Female*. Philadelphia: W.B. Saunders, 1953.
187. Klein, V. *The Feminine Character*. London: Kegan Paul, 1946.
188. Koblitz, A.H. Science, Women and the Revolution in Russia. *Science for the People* 14 (July–August 1982):14–18, 34.
189. Kolata, G.B. Sex Hormones and Brain Development. *Science* 205 (1979):985–987.
190. ———. Math Genius May Have a Hormonal Basis. *Science* 222 (1983): p. 1312.
191. Konishi, M., and Gurney, M.E. Sexual Differentiation of Brain and Behaviour. *Trends in Neurosciences* 5 (1982):20–23.
192. Lacoste-Utamsing, C. de, and Holloway, R.L. Sexual Dimorphism in the Human Corpus Callosum. *Science* 216 (1982):1431–1432.
193. La Fontaine, J.S., ed. *Sex and Age as Principles of Social Differentiation*. New York: Academic Press, 1978.
194. *Lancet*. Premenstrual Syndrome. Lancet, 19 December 1981, 1393–1394.
195. Larsen, R. Les fondements évolutionnistes des différences entre les sexes. In *Le fait féminin*, edited by E. Sullerot, 337–358. Paris: Fayard,

1978.

196. Lee, A.   Data for the Problem of Evolution in Man: A First Study of the Correlation of the Human Skulls. *Philosophical Transactions of the Royal Society of London* 196A (1902):225–264.

197. Léger, D.   *Le féminisme en France.* Paris: Le Sycomore, 1982.

198. Lempérière, T.; Ades, J.; and Ferrand, I.   A propos de l'épidémiologie des états dépressifs et de la vulnérabilité de la femme à la dépression. In *Entretiens de Bichat, 1979/Série Médicale,* 397–400. Paris: Expansion Scientifique Française, 1979.

199. Lemsine, A.   *Ordalie des voix: les femmes arabes parlent.* Paris: Encre, 1983.

200. Lepori, N.G.   *Sex Differentiation, Hermaphroditism and Intersexuality in Vertebrates Including Man.* London: Global Book Resources, 1981.

201. Le Rider, J.   *Le cas Otto Weininger: racines de l'antiféminisme et de l'antisémitisme.* Paris: Presses Universitaires de France, 1982.

202. Lerner, G.   Women in History. *Journal of American History* 69 (1982):7–20.

203. *Les femmes dans une société d'inégalités.* La Documentation Française, 1982.

204. Levitin, T.E.; Quinn, R.P.; and Staines, G.L.   A Woman is 58% of a Man. *Psychology Today* 6 (1973):89–91.

205. Levy, J.   Cerebral Asymmetry and the Psychology of Man. In *The Brain and Psychology,* edited by M.C. Wittrock, 245–321. New York: Academic Press, 1980.

206. ————.   Varieties of Human Brain Organization and the Human Social System, *Zygon* 15 (1980):351–375.

207. Lilar, S.   *Le malentendu du deuxième sexe.* Paris: Presses Universitaires de France, 1970.

208. Lloyd, C.B., and Niemi, B.T.   *The Economics of Sex Differentials.* New York: Columbia University Press, 1979.

209. Lombroso, G.   *L'âme de la femme.* Paris: Payot, 1923. (Trans. Le Hénaff.)

210. Love, R.   Alice in Eugenics-Land: Feminism and Eugenics in the Scientific Careers of Alice Lee and Ethel Elderton. *Annals of Science* 36 (1979):145–158.

211. Luchins, E.M., and Luchins, A.S.   Mathematical Ability: Is Sex a Factor? *Science* 212 (1981):117–118.

212. Lumsden, C.J., and Wilson, E.O.   *Genes, Mind, and Culture: The Coevolutionary Process.* Cambridge, Mass.: Harvard University Press, 1981.

213. Lumsden, C.J., and Wilson E.O.   *Promethean Fire: Reflections on the Origin of Mind.* Cambridge, Mass.: Harvard University Press, 1983.

214. Luria, Z.   Genre et étiquetage: l'effet Pirandello. In *Le fait féminin,* edited by E. Sullerot, 233–241. Paris: Fayard, 1978.

215. Luukkonen-Gronow, T., and Stolte–Heiskanen, V.   Myths and Realities of Women Scientists. *Acta Sociologica* 26 (1983):267–280.

216. Maccoby, E.E., and Jacklin, C.N. *The Psychology of Sex Differences*. 2 vols. Stanford: Stanford University Press, 1974.
217. Mackenzie, D. Karl Pearson and the Professional Middle Class. *Annals of Science* 36 (1979):125–143.
218. MacLusky, N.J., and Naftolin, F. Sexual Differentiation and the Central Nervous System. *Science* 211 (1981):1294–1303.
219. Malcolm, S.M. Women/Minorities in Science and Technology. *Science* 214 (1981):p. 135.
220. Manthorpe, C. Feminists Look at Science. *New Scientist* 105 (7 March 1985):29–31.
221. Maranto, G., and Brownlee, S. Why Sex? *Discover* 5 (February 1984):24–28.
222. Martin, P.Y. "Fair Science": Test or Assertion? A Response to Cole's "Women in Science." *Sociological Review* 30 (1982):478–508.
223. Maruani, M. *Les Syndicats à l'épreuve du féminisme*. Paris: Editions Syros, 1979.
224. Marx, J.L. Autoimmunity in Left-Handers. *Science* 217 (1982):141–144.
225. Marx, K., and Engels, F. *Lettres sur les sciences de la nature (et les mathématiques)*. Translated by J.P. Lefebvre. Paris: Editions Sociales, 1973.
226. Masica, D.N.; Money, J.; Ehrhardt, A.A.; and Lewis, V.G. IQ, Fetal Sex Hormones and Cognitive Patterns: Studies in the Testicular Feminizing Syndrome and Androgen Insensitivity. *Johns Hopkins Medical Journal* 124 (1969):34–43.
227. Matthaei, J.A. *An Economic History of Women in America: Women's Work, the Sexual Division of Labor and the Development of Capitalism.* New York: Schocken Books, 1982.
228. McCall, J.R. *Sex Differences in Intelligence: A Comparative Factor Study*. Washington: Catholic University of America Press, 1955.
229. McEwen, B.S. Sexual Differentiation of the Brain. *Nature* 291 (1981):p. 10.
230. ———. Neural Gonadal Steroid Actions. *Science* 211 (1981):1303–1311.
231. ———. Steroids and Brain Function. *Trends in Pharmacological Sciences* 6 (January 1985):22–25.
232. McGee, M.G. Human Spatial Abilities: Psychometric Studies and Environmental, Genetic, Hormonal and Neurological Influences. *Psychological Bulletin* 86 (1979):889–918.
233. McGlone, J. Sex Differences in Human Brain Asymmetry: A Critical Survey. *The Behavioral and Brain Sciences* 3 (1980):215–263.
234. McGuinness, D. Sex Differences in the Organization of Perception and Cognition. In *Exploring Sex Differences*, edited by B. Lloyd and J. Archer, 123–156. New York: Academic Press, 1976.
235. Mead, M. *Coming of Age in Samoa*. New York: William Morrow, 1928.

236. Merchant, C. *The Death of Nature: Women, Ecology and the Scientific Revolution*. San Francisco: Harper and Row, 1980.

237. Meyers, N. Israel's Women of Science. *Nature* 306 (1983):p. 104.

238. Michael, R.P., and Zumpe, D. Rhythmic Changes in the Copulatory Frequency of Rhesus Monkey (Macaca Mulatta) Under Laboratory Conditions. *Journal of Endocrinology* 40 (1970):231–246.

239. Michel, A. *Le féminisme*. 4th ed. Paris: Presses Universitaires de France/Collection Que sais-je?, 1980.

240. Mill, J. S. *The Subjection of Women*. Edited by S.M. Okin. Indianapolis and Cambridge: Hackett Publishing Co., 1988. (Orig. ed. 1869.)

241. Millett, K. *Sexual Politics*. New York: Doubleday, 1970.

242. Minces, J. *La femme dans le monde arabe*. Paris: Mazarine, 1980.

243. Mitchell, G. *Human Sex Differences: A Primatologist Perspective*. New York: Van Nostrand Reinhold, 1981.

244. Moebius, P.J. *De la débilité mentale physiologique chez la femme*. Translated by N.S. Roche. Paris: Solin, 1980. (Orig. ed. 1906.)

245. Mohan, J.; Sehgal, M.; and Bhandari, A. Intelligence, Sex and Vigilance. *Personality and Individual Differences* 3 (1982):343–344.

246. ———. Intelligence, Sex and Psychomotor Performance. *Personality and Individual Differences* 3 (1982):457–459.

247. Money, J. *Love and Love Sickness: The Science of Sex, Gender Difference and Pair-Bonding*. Baltimore: Johns Hopkins University Press, 1980.

248. ———, and Ehrhardt, A.A. Gender Dimorphic Behavior and Fetal Sex Hormones. *Recent Progress in Hormone Research* 28 (1972):735–754.

249. Moran, D.J. Mathematical Ability: Is Sex a Factor? *Science* 212 (1981): p. 115.

250. Moreau, T. *Le sang de l'histoire: Michelet, l'histoire et l'idée de la femme au XIXe siècle*. Paris: Flammarion, 1982.

251. Morin, F.-E. *La rouge différence*. Paris: Le Seuil, 1982.

252. Mosse, C. *La femme dans la Grèce antique*. Paris: Albin Michel, 1983.

253. Murphy, R.J.L. Sex Differences in Objective Test Performance. *British Journal of Educational Psychology* 52 (1982):213–219.

254. Myer, P. Women Executives are Different. *Dun's Review* 105 (1975):47–48.

255. Naftolin, F. Understanding the Bases of Sex Differences. *Science* 211 (1981):1263–1264.

256. Newcombe, N.; Bandura, M.M.; and Taylor, D.G. Sex Differences in Spatial Ability and Spatial Activities. *Sex Roles* 9 (1983):377–386.

257. *New Scientist*: Women Are Different. *New Scientist* 105 (21 February 1985):p. 16.

258. Nicholson, J. *Men and Women: How Different Are They?* Oxford and New York: Oxford University Press, 1984.

259. Nishizuka, M., and Arai, Y. Synapse Formation in Response to Estrogen in the Medial Amygdala Developing in the Eye. *Proceedings of the National Academy of Sciences* 79 (1983):7024–7026.

260. Nordeen, E.J., and Yahr, P. Hemispheric Asymmetries in the Behavioral and Hormonal Effects of Sexually Differentiating Mammalian Brain. *Science* 218 (1982):391–394.
261. Norris, R.V., and Sullivan, C. *PMS: Premenstrual Syndrome.* Rawson Assoc., 1983.
262. Norwood, J.L. *The Female-Male Earnings Gap: A Review of Employment and Earning Issues.* Report 673. Washington, D.C.: U.S. Department of Labor, Bureau of Labor Statistics, 1982.
263. Nyborg, H. Spatial Ability in Men and Women: Review and New Theory. *Advances in Behavioral Research Therapy* 5 (1983):89–140.
264. O'Leary, V.E.; Unger, R.K.; and Wallston, B.S.; eds. *Women, Gender, and Social Psychology.* Hillsdale: Lawrence Erlbaum, 1985.
265. O'Neill, W.L. Women in Politics. In *Female Hierarchies*, edited by L. Tiger and H. Fowler. Chicago: Beresford Book Service, 1978.
266. Osborne, R.T.; Noble, C.E.; and Weyl, N.; eds. *Human Variation.* New York: Academic Press, 1978.
267. Over, R. Representation of Women on the Editorial Boards of Psychology Journals. *American Psychologist* 36 (1981):885–891.
268. Paquot, E., ed. *Terre des femmes: panorama de la situation des femmes dans le monde.* Paris: La Découverte/Maspero, 1982.
269. Parsons, J.E., ed. *The Psychobiology of Sex Differences and Sex Roles.* New York: McGraw-Hill, 1980.
270. Patterson, M.A. Women in Management: An Experimental Study of the Effects of Sex and Marital Status on Job Performance Ratings, Promotability Ratings and Promotion Decisions. *Dissertation Abstracts International* 36 (1975):3108–3109 B.
271. Pearson, R. Women in Science and Engineering. *Nature* 315 (1985): p. 84.
272. Pelletier, A. *La femme dans la société gallo-romaine.* Paris: Picard, 1985.
273. Pelletier, M. *Nous sommes toutes responsables.* Paris: Stock, 1981.
274. Pezzulo, T.R., and Brittingham B.E., eds. *Salary Equity.* Lexington, Mass.: Lexington Books, 1979.
275. Pfaff, D.W. *Estrogens and Brain Function: Neural Analysis of a Hormone-Controlled Mammalian Reproductive Behavior.* New York: Springer-Verlag, 1980.
276. Pfafflin, S.M. Women, Science and Technology. *American Psychologist* 39 (1984):1183–1186.
277. Pfeiffer, J. Girl Talk, Boy Talk. *Science 1985* 6 (February 1985):58–63.
278. Philips, S.U. Sex differences and language. *Annual Review of Anthropology* 9 (1980):523–544.
279. Piret, R. *Psychologie différentielle des sexes.* 2d ed. Paris: Presses Universitaires de France, 1973.
280. Pleck, J.H. *The Myth of Masculinity.* Cambridge, Mass.: MIT Press, 1983.
281. Plomin, R., and Foch, T.T. Sex Differences and Individual Differences.

Child Development 52 (1981):383–385.

282. Potts, D.M. Which is the Weaker Sex? *Journal of Biosocial Science*, 1970, Suppl. 2:147–197.

283. Purtilo, D.T., and Sullivan, J.L. Immunological Bases for the Superior Survival of Females. *American Journal of Diseases of Children* 133 (1979):1251–1253.

284. Rae-Grant, Q. Women and Depression. *Canadian Journal of Psychiatry* 26 (1981):1–2.

285. Rainbow, T.C.; Parsons, B.; and McEwen, B.S. Sex Differences in Rat Brain Estrogen and Progestin Receptors. *Nature* 300 (1982):648–649.

286. Rashedi, K. *Les femmes en Iran avant et après la révolution*. Nouvelles Editions Rupture, 1983.

287. Reed, E. *Féminisme et anthropologie*. Paris: Denoël-Gonthier, 1979.

288. Reid., I., and Wormald, E., eds. *Sex Differences in Britain*. Grant McIntyre, 1982.

289. Reid, P.T. Feminism versus Minority Group Identity: Not for Black Women Only. *Sex Roles* 10 (1984):247–255.

290. Reskin, B.F., ed. *Sex Segregation in the Workplace: Trends, Explanations, Remedies*. Washington: National Academy Press, 1984.

291. Richter, D., ed. *Women Scientists*. London: Macmillan, 1982.

292. Roberts, H., ed. *Doing Feminist Research*. London: Routledge and Kegan Paul, 1981.

293. Roby, P. *Women in the Workplace: Proposals for Research and Policy Concerning the Conditions of Women in Industrial and Service Jobs*. Cambridge, Mass.: Schenkman, 1981.

294. Rocheblave, A.-M. *Les rôles masculins et féminins*. Paris: Editions Universitaires, 1970.

295. Rohrbaugh, J.B. *Women: Psychology's Puzzle*. New York: Basic Books, 1979.

296. Rosaldo, M.Z., and Lamphere, L. Editor's Introduction. In *Woman, Culture and Society*. Stanford: Stanford University Press, 1974.

297. Rose, R.M.; Holaday, J.W.; and Bernstein, I.S. Plasma Testosterone, Dominance Rank, and Aggressive Behavior in Male Rhesus Monkeys. *Nature* 231 (1971):366–368.

298. Rosenberg, R. *Beyond Separate Spheres: Intellectual Roots of Modern Feminism*. New Haven: Yale University Press, 1982.

299. Rossi, A. Equality Between the Sexes: An Immodest Proposal. *Daedalus* 93 (1964):607–652.

300. ———. A Biosocial Perspective on Parenting. *Daedalus* 106 (1977):1–32.

301. Rossi A.S. *Feminists in Politics: A Panel Analysis of the First National Women's Conference*. New York: Academic Press, 1982.

302. Rossiter, M. *Women Scientists in America: Struggles and Strategies to 1940*. Baltimore and London: Johns Hopkins University Press, 1982.

303. Rossiter, M.W. "Women's Work" in Science. *Isis* 71 (1980):381–398.

304. Rothschild, J., ed. *Women, Technology and Innovation*. London:

Pergamon, 1983.

305. Rousseau, R. *Les femmes rouges*. Paris: Albin Michel.

306. Royer, C. *Préface de la première édition de C. Darwin: de l'origine des espèces*. Paris: Flammarion, 1862, pp. I.–L.

307. ———. *Origine de l'homme et des sociétés*. Paris, 1870.

308. ———. *Théorie de l'impôt ou la dime sociale*. 2 vols. Paris: Guillaumin, 1962.

309. Rubin-Rabson, G. The Place of Women in Psychology. *American Psychologist* 37 (1982):866–867.

310. Rubin, R.T.; Reinisch, J.M.; and Haskett, R.F. Postnatal Gonadal Steroid Effects on Human Behavior. *Science* 211 (1981):1318–1324.

311. Ruble, T.L.; Cohen, R.; and Ruble, D.N. Sex Stereotypes: Occupational Barriers for Women. *American Behavioral Scientist* 27 (1984):339–356.

312. Rudolph, E.D. Women in 19th Century American Botany. *American Journal of Botany* 69 (1982):1346–1355.

313. Ruse, M. *Is Science Sexist? And Other Problems in the Biological Sciences*. London: Reidel, 1981.

314. Sabbah, F.A. *Woman in the Muslim Unconscious*. Oxford: Pergamon, 1984.

315. Sabrosky, J.A. *From Rationality to Liberation: The Evolution of Feminist Ideology*. London and Westport: Greenwood Press, 1980.

316. Samuel, W. Sex Differences in Spatial Ability Reflected in Performance on 10 Subtests by Black or White Examinees. *Personality and Individual Differences* 4 (1983):219–221.

317. Sanger, M. The Civilizing Force of Birth Control. In *Sex in Civilization*, edited by V.F. Calverton and S.D Schmalhausen, 525–537. New York: Garden City, 1929.

318. ———. *Margaret Sanger: An Autobiography*. New York: Dover Press, 1971. (Orig. ed. 1938.)

319. Sartre, J.-P. *L'être et le néant*. Paris: 1943.

320. Sayers, J. *Biological Politics: Feminist and Anti-Feminist Perspectives*. London and New York: Tavistock, 1982.

321. Scarf, M. *Unfinished Business*. New York: Ballantine Books, 1981. (Orig. ed. 1980.)

322. Schafer, A.T. Association for Women in Mathematics. *Science for the People* 13 (September-October 1981):p. 33.

323. ———, and Gray, M.W. Sex and Mathematics. *Science* 211 (1981):p. 229.

324. Scharf, L., and Jensen, J.M., eds. *Decades of Discontent: The Women's Movement, 1920–1940*. Westport, Conn.: Greenwood Press, 1983.

325. Schreiner, O. *Woman and Labor*. New York: Frederick A. Stokes, 1911.

326. Schwidetzky, I. von, and Spiegel-Rosing, I.S. Womanpower in der Anthropologie. *Homo* 31 (1980):232–236.

327. Scott, J.W. Les femmes et la mécanisation du travail. *Pour la Science*,

November 1982, 108–119.

328. Seward, J.P., and Seward, G.H. *Sex Differences: Mental and Temperamental.* Lexington, Mass.: Lexington, 1980.

329. Shanab, M.E., and Mcclure, F.H. Age and Sex Differences in Discrimination Learning. *Bulletin of the Psychonomic Society* 21 (1983):387–390.

330. Shanan, J., and Sagiv, R. Sex Differences in Intellectual Performance During Middle Age. *Human Development* 25 (1982):24–33.

331. Sharp, C. Physiology and the Woman Athlete. *New Scientist* 103 (2 August 1984):22–24.

332. Shaw, E., and Darling, J. *Strategies of Being Female.* London: Harvester.

333. Sheppard, R. Intelligence and Gender. *Atlas World Press Review* 26 (1979):p. 54.

334. Sheridan, E.M. *Sex Differences and Reading.* Delaware: International Reading Association, 1978.

335. Sherman, J. Girls' and Boys' Enrollments in Theoretical Math Courses: A Longitudinal Study, *Psychology of Woman Quarterly* 5 (1981):681–689.

336. Sherman, J.A., ed. *Sex-Related Cognitive Differences.* Springfield: C.C. Thomas, 1978.

337. Shields, S.A. Functionalism, Darwinism and the Psychology of Women: A Study of Social Myth. *American Psychologist* 30 (1975):739–754.

338. Shields, W.M. *Philopatry, Inbreeding and the Evolution of Sex.* New York: State University of New York Press, 1982.

339. Shock, N.W. Les caractéristiques biologiques et physiologiques du vieillissement chez les hommes et chez les femmes. *Adaptabilité et vieillissement: 9ᵉ Conférence Internationale de Gérontologie Sociale.* Quebec, Canada, 27–29 August 1980. Paris: CIGS, vol. 2, pp. 9–28.

340. Short, R.V. Sexual Selection and its Component Parts, Somatic and Genital, as Illustrated by Man and the Great Apes. In *Advances in the Study of Behaviour*, edited by J.S. Rosenblatt, R.A. Hinde, C. Beer and M.-C. Busnel. London: Academic Press, 1979.

341. Shucard, J.L.; Shucard, D.W.; Cummins, K.R.; and Campos, J.J. Auditory Evoked Potentials and Sex-Related Differences in Brain Development. *Brain and Language* 13 (1981):91–102.

342. Shuchman, H. A Science Policy for Women. *New Scientist* 103 (20 September 1984):33–36.

343. Shute, G.E.; Howard, M.M.; and Steyaert, J.P. The Relationships among Cognitive Development, Locus of Control, and Gender. *Journal of Research in Personality* 18 (1984):335–341.

344. Smith, M.J. *The Evolution of Sex.* London: Cambridge University Press, 1978.

345. Spence, J.T., and Helmreich, R.L. *Masculinity and Femininity.* Austin and London: University of Texas Press, 1978.

346. Spender, D. *Men's Studies Modified: The Impact of Feminism on the Academic Disciplines.* Pergamon: 1981.
347. Spiro, M.E. *Gender and Culture: Kibbutz Women Revisited.* Durham, N.C.: Duke University Press, 1979.
348. Stage, E.K., and Karplus, R. Mathematical Ability: Is Sex a Factor? *Science* 212 (1981):p. 114.
349. Stassinopoulos, A. *The Female Woman.* London: Davis-Poynter, 1973.
350. Stillion, J.M. Perspectives on the Sex Differential in Death. *Death Education* 8 (1984):237–256.
351. Sullerot, E., ed. *Le fait féminin.* Paris: Fayard, 1978.
352. ———. *La femme dans le monde moderne.* Paris: Hachette, 1974.
353. Sutherland, E.H., and Cressey, D.R. *Criminology.* 9th ed. Philadelphia: Lippincott, 1974. (Orig. ed. 1924.)
354. Sutton, C. A Role Model for Female Physicists. *New Scientist* 103 (13 September 1984):p. 53.
355. Swaab, D.F., and Fliers, E. A Sexually Dimorphic Nucleus in the Human Brain. *Science* 228 (1985):1112–1115.
356. Symons, D. *The Evolution of Human Sexuality.* New York: Oxford University Press, 1979.
357. ———. Y a-t-il une différence de nature entre l'homme et la femme? (Conversation with S. Keen.) *Psychologie,* June 1981, 35–40.
358. Tamborini, A. (interview with). "Souvent femme varie..." La preuve par les hormones. *Le Quotidien du Médecin,* 10 December 1984, 16–17.
359. Tannahill, R. *Le sexe dans l'histoire.* Paris: Robert Laffont, 1983. (Orig. ed. 1980.)
360. Tanner, N. *On Becoming Human.* London: Cambridge University Press, 1981.
361. Tavris, C., and Offir, C. *The Longest War: Sex Differences in Perspective.* New York: Harcourt Brace Jovanovich, 1977.
362. Terman, L.M., and Miles, C.C. *Sex and Personality: Studies in Masculinity and Femininity.* New York: McGraw-Hill, 1936.
363. Thibault, O. *Debout les femmes.* Lyon: Chronique Sociale, 1980.
364. Thomas, H. Familial Correlational Analyses, Sex Differences, and the X-Linked Gene Hypothesis. *Psychological Bulletin* 93 (1983):427–440.
365. Tiger, L. *Men in Groups.* New York: Random House, 1969.
366. ———, and Shepher, J. *Women in the Kibbutz.* New York: Harcourt Brace Jovanovich, 1975.
367. Tobach, E., and Rosoff, B. eds. *Genes and Gender.* New York: Gordian Press, 1978.
368. Tobias, S. *Le mythe des maths.* Paris and Montreal: Etudes Vivantes, 1980. (Orig. ed. 1978.)
369. Tomizuka, C., and Tobias, S. Mathematical Ability: Is Sex a Factor? *Science* 212 (1981):p. 114.
370. Trotman, S.C.A., and Hammond, G.R. Sex Differences in Task-Dependent EEG Asymmetries. *Psychophysiology* 16 (1979):429–431.
371. Valenza, C. Was Margaret Sanger a Racist? *Familial Planning*

Perspectives 17 (1985):44–46.

372. Velle, W. Sex Differences in Intelligence: Implications for Educational Policy. *Journal of Human Evolution* 13 (1984):109–115.
373. Vetter, B.M. Women Scientists and Engineers: Trends in Participation. *Science* 214 (1981):1313–1321.
374. Walden, R., and Walkerdine, V. *Girls and Mathematics: From Primary to Secondary.* London: University of London Institute of Education, 1985.
375. Wallon, G.H. *Les notions morales chez l'enfant: essai de psychologie différentielle (filles et garçons).* Paris: Presses Universitaires de France, 1949.
376. Warren, M.Q. *Comparing Female and Male Offenders.* London: Sage, 1981.
377. Weintraub, P. The Brain: His and Hers. *Discover* 2 (1981):14–20.
378. Weissman, M.M., and Klerman, G.L. Gender and Depression. *Trends in Neurosciences* 8 (1985):416–420.
379. ———, and Paykel, E.S. *The Depressed Woman: A Study of Social Relationships.* Chicago: University of Chicago Press, 1974.
380. Weitz, S. *Sex Roles: Biological, Psychological and Social Foundations.* New York: Oxford University Press, 1977.
381. Wellman, B.L. Sex Differences. In *A Handbook of Child Psychology* (2d ed.), edited by C. Murchinson. Worcester, Mass.: Clark University Press, 1933.
382. Werdelin, I. *Geometrical Ability and the Space Factor in Boys and Girls.* Lund, Sweden: University of Lund, 1961.
383. White, M.C.; De Sanctis, G.; and Crino, M.D. Achievement, Self-Confidence, Personality Traits, and Leadership Ability: A Review of the Literature on Sex Differences. *Psychological Reports* 48 (1981):547–569.
384. White, M.S. Psychological and Social Barriers to Women in Science. *Science* 170 (1970):413–416.
385. Whiting, B.B., and Edwards, C.P. A Cross-Cultural Analysis of Sex Differences in the Behavior of Children Aged Three through Eleven. *Journal of Social Psychology* 91 (1973):171–188.
386. Willerman, L. *The Psychology of Individual and Group Differences.* San Francisco: Freeman, 1979.
387. Williams, G.C. *Sex and Evolution.* Princeton, N.J.: Princeton University Press, 1975.
388. Williams, J.E.; Best, D.L.; Tilquin, C.; Keller, H.; Voss, H.-G.; Bjerke, T.; and Baarda, B. Traits Associated with Men and Women. *Journal of Cross-Cultural Psychology* 12 (1981):327–346.
389. Wilson, E.O. *Sociobiology: The New Synthesis.* Cambridge, Mass.: The Belknap Press, 1975.
390. ———. *On Human Nature.* Cambridge, Mass.: Harvard University Press, 1978.
391. Wilson, G. The Sociobiology of Sex Differences. *Bulletin of the British*

Psychological Society 32 (1979):350–353.
392. ———. *Love and Instinct.* London: Temple Smith, 1981.
393. Wilson, J.D.; George, F.W.; and Griffin, J.E. The Hormonal Control of Sexual Development. *Science* 211 (1981):1278–1284.
394. Wilson, J.D.; Griffin, J.E.; George, F.W.; and Leshin, M. The Role of Gonadal Steroids in Sexual Differentiation. *Recent Progress in Hormone Research* 37 (1981):1–33.
395. Wilson, M., and Daly, M. Competitiveness, Risk Taking and Violence: The Young Male Syndrome. *Ethology and Sociobiology* 6 (1985):59–73.
396. Wingard, D.L. The Sex Differential in Morbidity, Mortality, and Lifestyle. *Annual Review of Public Health* 5 (1984):433–458.
397. Witelson, S. Les différences sexuelles dans la neurologie de la cognition: implications psychologiques, sociales, éducatives et cliniques. In *Le fait féminin*, edited by E. Sullerot, 287–303. Paris: Fayard, 1978.
398. Wittig, M.A., and Petersen, A.C., eds. *Sex-Related Differences in Cognitive Functioning: Developmental Issues.* New York: Academic Press, 1979.
399. Zazzo, R. *Psychologie différentielle de l'adolescence.* Paris: Presses Universitaires de France, 1972.
400. ———. Quelques constats sur la psychologie différentielle des sexes. In *Le fait féminin*, edited by E. Sullerot, 263–272. Paris: Fayard, 1978.
401. Zwang, G. *La fonction érotique.* 2 vols. Paris: R. Laffont, 1976.

Index

Aggression, 39–40
Agnesi, Marie Gaetane, 72n
Agrippina, 37
Alexander, Richard, 36
Andersson, Malte, 32n
Anne of Austria, 53
Aquino, Corazon, 53

Babbage, Charles, 73n
Bach, Johann Sebastian, 76
Badinter, Elizabeth, 57, 105
Barash, David, 36
Baudelaire, Charles, 104
Beach, Frank, 36
Beaugé, Florence, 104
Beauvoir, Simone de, 1, 2, 31, 37, 101–104,
    107, 111–114
Benbow, Camilla, 72, 83
Benedict, Ruth, 99
Besant, Annie, 14
Bhutto, Benazir, 53
Bischof, Norbert, 31, 62
Blanche of Castille, 53
Blandine, 37
Blumberg, Samuel, 24
Bock, R.D., 69–70
Boesch, Christophe, 77
Boesch, Hedwinge, 77
Bouchardeau, Huguette, 53
Bouthoul, Gaston, 55
Brontë sisters, 37
Bushmen, 59
Burley, Nancy, 47
Burton, Frances, 36
Byron, Ada, 73n

Catherine the Great, 37, 53
Cattell, J.M., 75
Cau, Jean, 3
Cavendish, Margaret, 97
Cerutti, 89
Chamorro, Violeta, 53

Champagne, D., 23
Châtelet, Emilie du, 97n
Chevalier–Skolnikoff, Suzanne, 36
Choquet–Bruhat, Yvonne, 75
Cleopatra, 37
Colette, 37
Commensalism, 46, 49
Copernicus, 97
Crick, Francis, 97n
Curie, Marie, 37, 75, 97

Dalton, Katharina, 90
Darwin, Charles, 11, 12, 31, 38, 40, 97, 105
Dearden, J., 55
Depression, 90–92
Descartes, 98
Dimorphism, sexual, 3, 44–45
Draper, Patricia, 59
Duverger, Maurice, 51
Dyer, Kenneth, 27

Easlea, Brian, 97, 98
Eaubonne, Françoise d', 1
Einstein, Albert, 97
Elderton, Ethel, 14, 16
Eleanor of Aquitaine, 37
Elizabeth I, 53
Ellis, Havelock, 11, 14, 74
Eponine, 37
Erasmus, 79
Erikson, Erik, 102–103
Escoffier–Lambiotte, C., 68

Feminism, fundamental contradiction of,
    62–63, 92–93, 117
Fliers, E., 66
Fossey, Diane, 99
Fourier, Charles, 98
Fox, Robin, 106
Franck, R.T., 89
Franklin, Rosalind, 97
Friedan, Betty, 37

Galileo, 97
Galton, Francis, 14, 15, 16
Gandhi, Indira, 53
Gauss, Carl Friedrich, 72n
Germain, Sophie, 72n
Geschwind, N., 82–83
Goethe, Johann, Wolfgang von, 76
Goldfoot, Donald, 36
Goodall, Jane, 99
Gorski, Roger, 67
Gouges, Olympe de, 37, 53
Goy, Robert, 60, 81
Goya, 76
Grande Mademoiselle, La, 53
Greer, Germaine, 19
Guillemin, Roger, 67

Hamilton, J.B., 25
Héloïse, 37
Hier, Daniel, 83
Hilbert, David, 73n
Homosexuality, 33–34
Hormones, male and female, 28, 29, 55–56,
    61, 81–85, 106, 115
Hrdy, Sarah Blaffer, 19, 35–36, 40–48, 96,
    99, 109–110
Hypatia, 72n

Imperato–McGinley, Julianne, 60, 82
Infanticide, 42–43, 45–46, 48
Isabella the Catholic, 53

Jacklin, Carol N., 39
Jarvik, I., 69
Joan of Arc, 37
Joliot–Curie, Irène, 37, 76, 97
Jost, Alfred, 30

Kaplan, Marcie, 92–93
Kerbaum, S., 23
Keyserling, Hermann, Graf, 95, 106–107
Kibbutz, 8, 59–60
Koestler, Arthur, 84
Kolakowski, D., 69–70
Kollman, J., 15
Kovalevski, Sonya, 73n

Lacoste–Utamsing, Christine de, 66, 68
Lafargue, Paul, 13
Laguillier, Arlette, 53
Lamphere, Louise, 49
Lancaster, Jane, 36, 99
Larsen, Roger, 56
Lee, Alice, 14–16, 18, 19
Lempérière, T., 91
Lenclos, Ninon de, 37

Leonardo da Vinci, 76
Letourneau, 14
Levy, Jerre, 78–79
L'Héritier, Françoise, 99
Lillie, Frank, 81
Liszt, Franz, 76
Lombroso, Cesare, 90
Longueville, Duchesse de, 53
Lorenz, Konrad, 42
Love, Rosaleen, 16
Lysenko, Trofim Denisovich, 1

McClintock, Barbara, 97, 100
Maccoby, Eleanor, 39
McEwen, Bruce, 66–67, 82, 92, 110
MacLean, Paul, 84
Maines, David, 71–72
Male dominance, 49–50, 54
Mall, F.P., 65
Marcuse, Herbert, 98
Maria Theresa, 53
Marx, Eleanor, 14
Marx, Karl, 11, 13, 14, 98
Mayr, Ernest, 31
Mead, Margaret, 35–36, 99
Medici, Catherine de', 37, 53
Medici, Marie de', 53
Meir, Golda, 53
Méricourt, Théroigne de, 53
Michael, Richard, 36
Michel, Louise, 53
Michelangelo, 76
Mill, John Stuart, 100–101
Mimoun, A., 27
Mitchell, G., 50
Moebius, P.J., 1
Molière, 76
Money, John, 61
Monod, Jacques, 110
Monogamy, 32, 44–45
Montesquieu, 17
Moos, R.H., 90
Morgan, Elaine, 36
Morris, Desmond, 36
Motherhood, 4–5, 13, 104–106

Natural selection, 37
Newton, Isaac, 97
Nietzsche, Friedrich, 21, 50
Noether, Emmy, 73n
Noether, Max, 73n
Noonan, Katherine, 36
Nottebohm, Fernando, 66
Nymphomania, 35, 46–48

O'Neill, William L., 52

Orgasm, 34–36

Pasteur, Louis, 97
Pauline, 37
Pearson, Karl, 14–16
Perón, Eva, 53
Plato, 49
Polygamy, 32, 44–45
Pompadour, Madame de, 37
Premenstrual syndrome, 89–90
Pugh, George, 36
Purtillo, David, 23–24
Pythagoras, 97n

Reed, Evelyn, 96
Roland, Madame, 53
Rosaldo, Michelle Zimbalist, 49
Rossi, Alice, 105
Royer, Clémence, 11–13, 18, 19

Sachs, Sadie, 17
Saint–Simon, Henri, comte de, 98
Sand, George, 37
Sanger, Margaret, 16–19
Sartre, Jean–Paul, 1, 98, 101, 107
Scarf, Maggie, 90–91, 109
Schally, Andrew, 67
Schmidberger, 73
Schmitt, Carl, 55
Schreiner, Olive, 14, 16
Ségur, Comtesse de, 37
Semiramis, 52
Sévigné, Marquise de, 37
Shakespeare, William, 76
Sharp, Craig, 28
Sociobiology, 38
Sommerville, Mary Fairfax, 72n
Spencer, Herbert, 4–5, 105
Spiro, Melford E., 59–60
Sports, 26–28
Stanley, Julian, 72, 83
Stassinopoulos, Arianna, 74, 117
Stereotypes, sexual, 9–10
Stern, Karl, 98
Strategy r and strategy K, 39
Struhsaker, Thomas, 43
Sullerot, Evelyne, 1, 70–71, 110, 111
Sullivan, John, 23–24
Swaab, D.F., 66
Symons, Donald, 32–36, 47

Tamborini, Alain, 90
Tazi, L., 23
Teresa of Avila, 76
Thatcher, Margaret, 53
Theon of Alexandria, 72n

Thibaut, Odette, 1
Tiger, Lionel, 53, 106
Tristan, Flora, 37
Turner, Sir William, 15

Victoria, 37
Victoria, Queen, 37, 53
Visscher, P. de, 76

Wagner, Richard, 76
Waitz, Grette, 26
Watson, James, 97n
Weierstrass, Karl, 73n
Weininger, Otto, 1
Wilson, Gleen, 34–35, 110
Wilson, Mrs., 14
Witelson, Sandra, 68–69, 78, 91
Woolf, Virginia, 37

Yallow, Rosalind, 97
Young, William, 81

Zumpe, Doris, 36
Zwang, Gérard, 30